AF431840

Born of the Spirit
Live in the Spirit
Walk in the Spirit
Pray in the Spirit
Free in the Spirit

Paul Talafo

Born of the Spirit
Live in the Spirit
Walk in the Spirit
Pray in the Spirit
Free in the Spirit

Job Daniel Jean

Other books from Paul Talafo:
- Vanquish and triumph in Jesus Christ
- Le disciple que Jésus-Christ cherche - *Au bon souvenir de Marie Madeleine*
- Les premiers seront les derniers et les derniers seront les premiers - *Qui sont-ils ?*
- Du sacerdoce lévitique au sacerdoce du Christ, la lumière sur le salut par la grâce au moyen de la foi - *Sur le fondement des apôtres et des prophètes*
- Un cœur brisé et contrit ou la repentance, la gratitude et la couronne des vainqueurs
- Les écluses des cieux aux héritiers de Dieu et cohéritiers avec Christ sur la terre en ce temps-ci

Unless otherwise indicated, all Scripture quotations are from the electronic Modern King James Version (eMKJV).

BORN OF THE SPIRIT, LIVE IN THE SPIRIT, WALK IN THE SPIRIT, PRAY IN THE SPIRIT, FREE IN THE SPIRIT

Paul Talafo, 2018

ISBN: 979-10-94949-11-5
Printed in the United States of America

Job Daniel Jean
Ministère chrétien pour l'enseignement
job.daniel.jean@gmail.com

This book is an English translation of the French book *Naître par l'Esprit, Vivre par l'Esprit, Marcher par l'Esprit, Prier par l'Esprit, Libérer par l'Esprit*

Table of contents

INTRODUCTION

We must recognize that the Holy Spirit is not as popular in religious circles as the words 'Lord', 'God' and 'Jesus Christ'. Yet Jesus Christ Himself affirmed the following:

> *«I will pray the Father, and He shall give you another Comforter, **so that He may be with you forever**, the Spirit of truth, whom the world cannot receive because it does not see Him nor know Him. But you know Him, for He dwells with you and shall be in you»* (**John 14:16-17**).

How can we ignore someone who is eternally with us and in us? It always amazes me. Is it because I have been very active in Pentecostal circles where gifts and ministries of the Holy Spirit abound? Possible. Is it because there is a lot of confusion and excess in the understanding of that name? Likely, because if there is indeed the Holy Spirit with upper 'S', there is also the human spirit in lower 's'. Many may even wonder whether we often do not take the human spirit for the Holy Spirit, or if we do not take our own will for that of God. We will push the controversy further by speaking of the falsifications of the gifts of the Spirit. If there are false spiritual gifts, it is conceivable that there is a spirit of falsehood that would pass for the Holy Spirit. The Scripture speaks explicitly about it. Jesus said indeed:

> «***False christs and false prophets*** *will arise and show great signs and wonders; so much so that, if it were possible, they would deceive even the elect*» (**Matthew 24:24**).

The Scripture thus evokes, towards the end of time, manipulations of miracles which can fool the saints.

Let's be relaxed. Confusion exists only in those who perish – those who do not know God. Christians should not be troubled if they keep the essential: the Word of God, the sword of the Spirit (**Ephesians 6:17, Revelation 1:16**). Only the Word of God is true. There is what the Scripture says and what the world says. The Word of God is true while that of the world passes like grass. The Lord has urged His Christians to keep His commandments because the Scripture is trustworthy.

The purpose of this book is to break the complex of Christians with regard to the Holy Spirit and His true role with them. If the Lord has promised the Holy Spirit by saying that He will be eternally with Christians, near them and in them, there is much to know about the Spirit. This is what we will try to understand through five essential truths emphasized in the scriptures: to be born of the

Spirit, to live in the Spirit, to walk in the Spirit, to pray in the Spirit and to free in the Spirit.

The words 'Christian', 'Disciple', 'Saint or Holy' will be considered perfectly equal, as well as 'Bible' and 'Scripture'.

We apologize to the reader for the redundancies and repetitions that will undoubtedly alter the style and beauty of the language. The concern to explain difficult truths by simple words made them necessary, even unavoidable.

Unless otherwise notice, all Bible quotations are from the Modern King James Version (MKJV). They are pasted in this book for a reason. **Matthew 5:10-13** means *the book of Matthew, chapter 5, verses 10 to 13*. For the sake of truth, we were careful to mention each Bible verse with respect to the historical context, highlighting the essential part in **bold**. The reader may find boring the full reproduction of Bible verses rather than footnotes. This was done on purpose because memorized verses tend to suffer discrepancies as time passes. Is it due to memory failure or evil action? We presume a bit of both. Is this why the Israelites, after a long period of obedience, began to transgress the commandments of God? Possible. We note that Moses instructed the Israelites to *bind the commandments for a sign upon their hand, as frontlets between their eyes, and to write them upon the posts of their house, and on their gates* (**Deuteronomy 6:8-9**). This warning of Moses is not fortuitous. The reader is therefore invited not to be exasperated with the reproduction of the Scriptures, but rather to read them studiously. He will notice that some verses which he thought he had memorized well, come in a different way. We have put in boxes very important notices. Finally, all the pronouns referring to the Lord God have been put in capital letter, for the sake of both accuracy and God's holiness. May the Lord God accompany you reader, open your mind and intelligence to seize the length and depth of His love for the men and women He approves of, in addition to His call to the first resurrection. Indeed *"Blessed and holy is he who has part in the **first resurrection**. The second death has no authority over these, but they will be priests of God and of Christ, and will reign with Him a thousand years"* (**Revelation 20:6**).

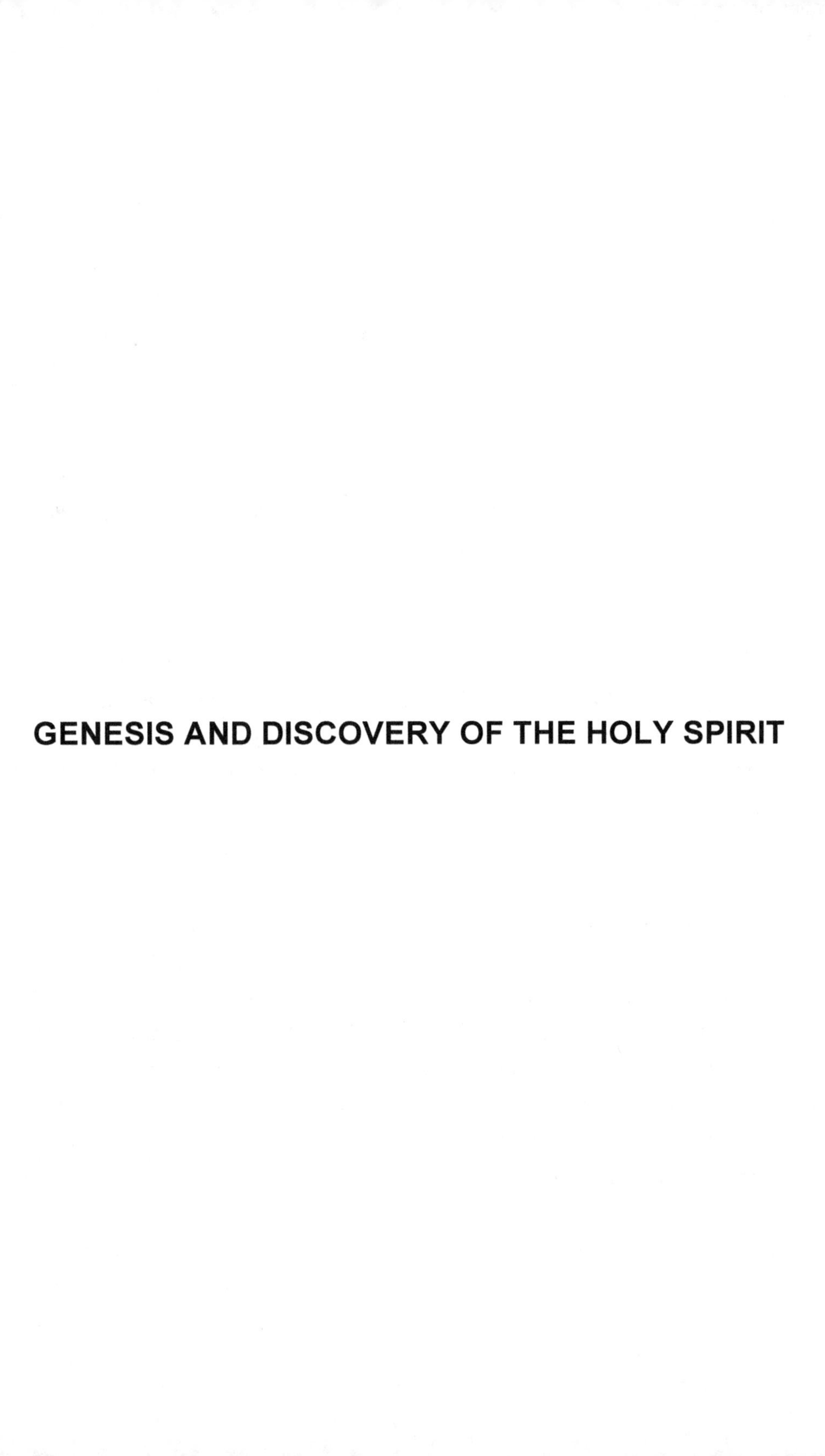

GENESIS AND DISCOVERY OF THE HOLY SPIRIT

Basic knowledge

- At creation, God endowed man with a natural spirit

> *«Jehovah God formed man of the dust of the ground, and breathed into his nostrils the breath of life; and man became a living soul»* **Genesis 2:7**.

The above verse attests to the earthly origin of man because he was formed of the dust of the earth. Originally, man was only an inert and lifeless mass. God made him live by breathing into his nostrils a vital breath. Concretely then, it is the breath of God that put the man in movement.

According to human physiology, we understand that the human body is irrigated by the blood pumped from its biological heart. How from the breath of God did man become the one described above? We understand that the original breath of God set in motion the biological heart and the blood. According to science, the blood starts from the biological heart, bright red because of the oxygen it carries, and returns in a loop, dark red because of the carbon dioxide collected throughout the circuit.

The original breath of God now maintains the biological heart from which blood comes and goes. It is this original breath that has become the human spirit. As this human spirit keeps the heart beating, it is also called the spiritual heart because it lives in the region of the biological heart, even though we can neither see nor scan it. Ultrasound and radiography give the image of the biological heart but not that of the spiritual heart which is the spirit of man. We will see later that it is in the spiritual heart – human spirit – that the Holy Spirit comes to dwell at the regeneration of the Christian: it is the new birth of the Christian – born again.

Let us remember, then, that the breath of God, at the origin of the creation of man of the dust, not only set the biological heart in motion, but also created the human spirit in the region of the biological heart. Wherever the Scripture speaks of the circumcision of the heart, it is about operations in the human spirit or spiritual heart. The introduction of the Holy Spirit into the human spirit, when the Christian comes to Jesus, is considered the circumcision of the spiritual heart, because the biological heart cannot be circumcised – extraction of the foreskin.

When someone is told that he has a good or bad heart, one speaks of the spiritual heart and not of the biological heart.

- The natural man is born of the flesh, lives and walks by the flesh

> «*But as many as received Him, He gave to them authority to become the children of God, to those who believe on His name, **who were born, not of bloods, nor of the will of the flesh, nor of the will of man**, but were born of God*» **John 1:12-13**.

All humans are born from the woman's placenta. The newborn is a perfectly constituted being with blood circulating in his veins. He is sometimes called the son of blood. Scripture and medicine confirm this reality by saying that man is born of the blood, of the will of the flesh, or of the will of man. It is customary to summarize these three possibilities in one: the flesh. Man is born of the flesh. The flesh is the engine of its existence.

Scripture says that "*life is in the blood*" (**Leviticus 17:11**), which is why God has always forbidden men to consume the blood, to shed the blood of his fellow men (**Genesis 9:5-6**). Edible animals could not be consumed with their blood. It was first necessary to spread their blood on the ground before consumption.

If the natural man is born of blood, we understand that the flesh is the driving force behind man's activity on earth. It is said that man lives and walks by blood. It is the blood that irrigates all veins of the human body. When a vein is not irrigated, the organ is inactive. This is the case of certain physical handicaps.

In short, man, from the placenta, is born of blood, lives and walks by the flesh.

- **The spiritual man is born of the Spirit, lives and walks in the Spirit**

Just as the natural man is born of the flesh, so the spiritual man – Christian – is born of the Spirit. The natural man comes from the earth, while the spiritual man comes from heaven. We must go back to genesis to establish a parallel between birth of the flesh and birth of the Spirit. Scripture explicitly states that Adam, the first man, came from the earth; that is why he became a living soul – by the blood. While the last Adam (Jesus), from heaven, became a life-giving spirit. It is indeed written:

> «*So also is it written: 'Adam, the first man, became a **living soul**'; the second Adam – Jesus – became a **quickening Spirit***» (**1 Corinthians 15:45/Murdoch Bible/1851**).

The first Adam reproduced on the earth by blood, through the placenta of women. While Jesus Christ multiplied Christian descent on the earth by the Holy Spirit who communicates life. This is why Jesus said to Nicodemus:

> «***Unless a man is born of water and the Spirit***, *he cannot enter into the kingdom of God*» (**John 3:5**).

Further on, Apostle Paul will declare:

> «*If anyone has not the Spirit of Christ, he is none of His*» (**Romans 8:9**).

Let's take a closer look at Nicodemus' concern when Jesus told him he had to be born again. He answered: "*How can a man be born when he is old? **Can he enter the second time into his mother's womb and be born?**"*(**John 3:4**). This is the essential point. The biological birth and the multiplication of the Adam's descent are done by the flesh, by the blood and by the will of men, while the new birth in Christ is done by the Spirit. There is no need for a descendant of Adam to return to his mother's womb to be spiritually begotten. How, then, does the Holy Spirit bring forth a new creature in Christ? **It is by invigorating the human spirit. He who receives the Holy Spirit in him, is quickened in his spirit. His human spirit is quickened by becoming the seat of the Holy Spirit.** This is the new birth in Christ.

> The new birth in Christ cannot be summed up either in the frequentation of Christian circles, in the imposition of the most secure hands, or in marriage with a Christian, although these three operations are important. The new birth in Christ begins as soon as the spirit of the natural man is touched (enlivened) by the Holy Spirit who establishes Himself there.

As much as he who is born of the flesh, now lives by the flesh and the blood that circulates in his veins, as much as he who is born of the Spirit, lives by the Spirit through the divine life communicated in his members. We will detail it later.

Scripture reminds us that the life of the natural man is in the blood. This is because the blood circulates and irrigates all the vessels of the human body. What about the Christian? The new life of the Christian is communicated in his limbs – mortal – by the Holy Spirit. The biological blood circulating in the Christian's limbs has nothing to do with the new life communicated by the Holy Spirit. Human blood communicates and maintains human life while the Holy Spirit communicates and maintains the new life, the divine life. The Scripture says:

> «*But if the Spirit of the One who raised up Jesus from the dead dwells in you, the One who raised up Christ from the dead **shall also make your mortal bodies alive by His Spirit who dwells in you***» (**Romans 8:11**).

Apostle Paul reveals in his Epistle to the Romans that the Holy Spirit communicates life to our mortal bodies. It is a divine life. The Holy Spirit, present in the human spirit, communicates the divine life to the rest of the body which is yet mortal. Warning: the presence of the Holy Spirit in the spirit of man does not make his members – physical body – immortal. Otherwise Christians would be immortal. On the other hand, the Holy Spirit will not go beyond His communicating the life of God to the human body – mortal. It is this divine life that operates through the human body according to the will of God. It was through this divine life that David was able, though as a teenager, to kill the lion and the bear, and later to kill General Goliath with a slingshot and stone. It was this divine life that allowed David to play the harp to appease King Saul in torment.

It is this divine life that fulfills the will of God through the mortal members of the Christian because, sooner or later, the Christian will return to God and his physical body will return to the dust. While waiting for this fatal issue, the life of the Spirit is communicated to the members of the Christian to fulfill the will of God.

The natural man – son of Adam – is born of the blood and lives in the flesh. The spiritual man – Christian – is born of the Spirit and lives in the Spirit.

If the natural man is born, lives and walks in the flesh, then the spiritual man is born of, lives and walks in the Spirit. This is the substance of Apostle Paul's exhortation:

> *«If we live in (born of) the Spirit, **let us also walk in the Spirit»*** (**Galatians 5:25**).

With these words, Apostle Paul recognizes that a Christian who is born and lives in the Spirit can err in walking in the flesh. Unfortunately, many Christians are always tempted to function as if they were of this world. They reproduce the life of pagans. The apostle invites to move away from the tendencies of the flesh. He warns that if a Christian walks in the flesh, he will die:

> *«**If you live according to the flesh, you shall die**. But if you through the Spirit mortify the deeds of the body, you shall live. For as many as are led by the Spirit of God, they are the sons of God»* (**Romans 8:13-14**).

Another way of differentiating between birth of the flesh and birth of the Spirit is to see that the biological heart of man circulates the blood in the various arteries of the body. It is God who, blowing into the nostrils of the first Adam – drawn from the dust of the ground – activated the first heartbeat. Since then, the natural man has reproduced by transmitting this faculty to his descendants. In launching the beats of the biological heart, God also created the human spirit: it is the original breath of God in the biological heart. So the human spirit or the spiritual heart of man should not be confused with the biological heart that is visible and palpable.

The spiritual heart or human spirit is the place occupied by the Holy Spirit at the regeneration of the Christian. It is said that the Christian is live-quickened, that he is born again. It is also said that the Christian's (spiritual) heart is circumcised. Throughout Scripture, when it comes to circumcision of the heart, it is related to the Spirit dwelling in the man's spirit. The Holy Spirit comes to dwell in the Christian by colonizing his human spirit. The spirit of the Christian is also his spiritual heart because, as indicated above, it is by the breath of God in the nostrils of man, that the biological heart began to beat. The biological heart can be considered as the location area of the human spirit. But one cannot physically circumcise the biological heart. However one can circumcise the spiritual heart by bringing the Holy Spirit into the human spirit.

Utility and role of the Holy Spirit

The Holy Spirit acts on all flesh, Christian and pagan altogether, as it is written, "*I will pour out of My Spirit **upon all flesh**"* (**Acts 2:16**). Jesus also states that the Holy Spirit upon His arrival *will* *convict the world concerning sin, and concerning righteousness, and concerning judgment* (**John 16:8**). We will highlight the various functions of the Holy Spirit by recalling that the Holy Spirit faithfully replaces Jesus Christ on earth, with the difference that the Holy Spirit remains invisible while Jesus of Nazareth was visible.

- As for the world: the Holy Spirit convicts of sin, justice and judgment

> «*And when that One (Holy Spirit) comes, **He will convict the world concerning sin, and concerning righteousness, and concerning judgment***» **John 16:8**.

Scripture does not allow us to go beyond the limits it sets itself in a literary style of its own. We would do well to stick to this discipline to avoid guilty diversions. The Scripture warns against any addition and withdrawal of truths. It is written, "*For I testify together to everyone who hears the words of the prophecy of this book: if anyone adds to these things, God will add on him the plagues that have been written in this book. And if anyone takes away from the words of the book of this prophecy, God will take away his part out of the book of life, and out of the holy city, and from the things which have been written in this book*" (**Revelation 22:18-19**). Through the verse **John 16:8** above, one can ask in all relevance how the Holy Spirit of God comes to convince sinners.

How will He proceed when we know that Jesus Christ promised the Holy Spirit only to those who believe in Him (**John 14:26**)?

The answer is provided by Scriptures. In the prophecy of Joel concerning the coming of the Holy Spirit, a prophecy recalled by Peter at Pentecost, we are told that God *will pour out of His Spirit upon ALL flesh* (**Acts 2:17**). Other Bible versions say: "**On ALL men**".

> «*And it shall be in the last days, says God,* ***I will pour out of My Spirit upon ALL flesh****. And your sons and your daughters shall prophesy, and your young men shall see visions, and your old men shall dream dreams. And in those days I will pour out My Spirit upon My slaves and My slave women, and they shall prophesy. And I will give wonders in the heaven above, and miracles on the earth below, blood and fire and vapor of smoke. The sun shall be turned into darkness and the moon into blood, before that great and glorious day of the Lord. And it shall be that everyone who shall call upon the name of the Lord shall be saved*» (**Acts 2:17-21**).

When Jesus Christ announces the coming of the Holy Spirit – Comforter – He says that the Holy Spirit will come **near** and **inside** His disciples. That is, the Holy Spirit will be outside (**near** or on the flesh/skin) and inside (in the human spirit) of the disciple:

> *«And I will pray the Father, and He shall give you another Comforter – Holy Spirit – so that He may be with you forever, (...) for He dwells **with you** and shall be **in you**»* (**John 14:16-17**).

By saying that the Holy Spirit will come to His disciples, Jesus is in tune with the prophet Joel. By affirming that the Holy Spirit will come into the disciple, Jesus predicts in advance the status of the believing Christian: the Christian is the temple of the Holy Spirit (**1 Corinthians 6:19**).

So today, according to the prophet Joel, every human being has the Holy Spirit on the flesh (skin), whatever his religion: Muslim, Atheist, Polytheist, Animist, etc. We specify "ON the skin/flesh" and not "IN the body/flesh". The role of the Holy Spirit is to *convict the world concerning sin, and concerning righteousness, and concerning judgment*. The Holy Spirit will know how to do it because He is present on ALL flesh/skin.

Towards the pagan, the Holy Spirit leads to guilt for eternal judgment – damnation – if the pagan does not repent. Towards the Christian, on the other hand, the Holy Spirit leads to glory *"But whom He predestinated (to be like the image of His Son), these He also called; and whom He called, those he also justified. And whom He justified, these He also **glorified**"* (**Romans 8:30**).

It is not for us to decipher how the Holy Spirit, present on all human flesh, proceeds to convict of sin, righteousness and judgment. Knowing that God has access to the heart of every man, to have breathed life into his nostrils in the beginning, there is no doubt about His ability to convince the pagan through His Spirit present on the skin of this pagan.

- **The Holy Spirit searches the depths of God with the Christian**

> «*The Spirit searches all things, yea, the deep things of God*» **1 Corinthians 2:10**.

This Scripture quotation indicates the propensity of the Holy Spirit to probe the depths of God. It is obvious, we say, because God is also Spirit. But two verses earlier, an affirmation is intriguing. The apostle says:

> «*But as it is written, 'eye has not seen, nor ear heard, nor has it entered into the heart of man'* **the things which God has prepared FOR those who love Him**» (**1 Corinthians 2:9**).

Clearly, when the Spirit searches the depths of God, being God Himself (explained below), we must understand that the Spirit does it **FOR** *those who love God*. It is precisely a visit to the inner rooms of God. It means concretely that God likes to show His inner rooms to those who love Him. Dear reader, should you not be a part of those who love God, since God desires you to visit His secret rooms?

What is found in the inner rooms of God? All. Absolutely everything. All that pertains to the creation of God in the heavens, on the earth, and in the waters below the earth. In all its variety therefore. In creating man in His image, God had no less ambition than to reveal Himself to this man as He is: God.

Which mother would not like to tell everything to her daughter? Which father would not like to reveal everything to his son? This is very important for preparing offspring to meet the challenges of the future. God does not think less. He wants His children to be equipped to meet all the challenges of life. He wants His children to know Him. Praying to His Father, Jesus said indeed:

> «*And this is life eternal, **that they might know You**, the only true God, and Jesus Christ Whom You have sent*» (**John 17:3**).

God will do everything for His children to know Him, as long as His children are willing and interested. As it comes from God and not from man, it is a gift. It is up to the man to reach out and not to miss such an important grace.

> To visit the inner rooms of God thanks to the Holy Spirit who searches the depths of God, brings the Christian to meet the inexpressible intentions of God on all questions of life. The longer this exercise continues in time, the more the Christian will know God and His will on different matters of existence.

Let the Christian, accustomed to this exercise, not be surprised by the instinctive reflexes he can have on truths and facts of society. It will happen that, without a rational explanation, the Christian feels inwardly strong opposition to an event, a thought, a behavior, an opinion. It is the result of his many walks in the inner rooms of God. It is after taking into consideration this opposition that God will give him a Scripture quotation.

This is why the Christian must never stop sanctifying himself. *Watch and pray!* Says the Lord. This spiritual watch includes continuous sanctification. Through this exercise, the Christian becomes accustomed to the will of God, who can first express himself by instinct, before an explanation based on Scripture.

The Anointing (Holy Spirit) we have received cannot lie. He is real. He is a very reliable teacher because Scripture says that we no longer need to be taught because Anointing teaches us everything. It is indeed written:

> «*But the Anointing which you received from Him abides in you, **and you do not need anyone to teach you.** But as His Anointing teaches you concerning all things, **and is true and no lie**, and as He has taught you, abide in Him*» (**1 John 2:27**).

- When does God reveal His depths to His children?

This question is fundamental but simple to deal with. Visiting the inner rooms of God has no fixed time. It is a total discretion of the Holy Spirit. The Holy Spirit will seize every opportunity to walk the Christian in the inner rooms of God. The purpose of these visits is to nourish, consolidate the communion, the conscience and the instinct of the Christian.

These visits can be done at any time of the day, during a round trip, during work, in the toilet or in the shower, during walks, during night watches. At all times when the Spirit and the Christian are ready to communicate.

The Holy Spirit can exhume a passage from the Scriptures if He believes the understanding of the Christian insufficient. As the Spirit searches all things, including the heart of the Christian, He perfectly measures the level of understanding that we have of the word of God. The Spirit has received from the Lord the mission to lead the Christian into all truth and to remind him of what Christ has taught:

> *«But the Comforter, the Holy Spirit Whom the Father will send in My name, He shall **teach you all things** and **bring all things to your remembrance, whatever I have said to you»** (**John 14:26**).

These moments can multiply to infinity. The Christian will then be able to measure the Lord's love for him through the Holy Spirit. For as much as parents teach their children, to assure them of a solid education, a sign of their parental love, so much, even more, the Spirit wants Christians to know God as well as the One whom He sent: Jesus Christ.

The Christian will realize, by himself, how the Spirit is tender, loyal and faithful in love. The touch of the Spirit is as sweet as oil – ointment – which is why it is assimilated to the anointing. Those who possess the Spirit of Christ know something about it. God loves His children perfectly.

By fortifying the communion, the conscience and the instinct of the Christian, the latter will know how to recognize the voice of His Master among a thousand. Jesus says indeed:

> *«When he (shepherd) puts forth his own sheep, he goes before them, and the sheep follow him. **For they know his voice. And they will not follow a stranger, but will flee from him, for they do not know the voice of strangers»*** (**John 10:4-5**).

> *«Behold, I (Jesus) stand at the door and knock. If anyone hears My voice and opens the door, I will come in to him and will dine with him and he with Me»* (**Revelation 3:20**).

Dinner is a time when souls speak calmly around a meal, often the most hearty of the day because after, it's a long night of rest. So we have time to talk freely, the daily constraints being reduced to a minimum. In targeting this time of the day of supper, the Lord indicates the seriousness with which He intends to discuss with His sheep all the relevant questions. The Lord adores these moments because He can then rebuke and encourage, as the case may be, for the edification of Christians to the glory of God the Father.

- **By visiting the depths of God, we hear the voice of God**

Before venturing into the depths of God, I had always been, like many Christians, curious about how God spoke to people. God indeed has many ways of speaking to His children. The visitation of

God's inner rooms is another way of hearing His voice. Whenever you face any situation, the touch of the Spirit, according to your experience of the depths of God, will be the sign that God has spoken to you. The more you practice visiting the inner rooms of God, the more you will know the will of God on different subjects of life. People will be curious to know how God speaks to you. God speaks, that's all.

Should we really ask ourselves how God speaks? God is His own Word who speaks – *In the beginning was the Word, and the Word was with God, **and the Word was God*** (**John 1: 1**). Is it not the very essence of the Word to emit? The Word emits the will of God since the beginning of all things, before things came into existence, all things. No need to be moved. It is obvious. God speaks. The Word emits. Just be in the right frequency to hear it. We are in the right frequency by visiting the depths of God through the Holy Spirit. Amen!

The Holy Spirit: Who is He truly?

- A Promise

The prophet Joel, relayed by Apostle Peter, announced the advent of the Holy Spirit in these terms:

> **«*And it shall be in the last days, says God, I will pour out of My Spirit upon all flesh*.** *And your sons and your daughters shall prophesy, and your young men shall see visions, and your old men shall dream dreams. And in those days I will pour out My Spirit upon My slaves and My slave women, and they shall prophesy. And I will give wonders in the heaven above, and miracles on the earth below, blood and fire and vapor of smoke»* (**Acts 2:16-21**).

Jesus confirmed by saying:

> **«*When the Comforter has come, whom I will send to you from the Father, the Spirit of truth*** *who proceeds from the Father, He shall testify of Me»* (**John 15:26**).

The Holy Spirit has indeed been promised long before Pentecost. We must never misunderstand the Holy Spirit, even though no one has seen Him with eyes. His advent was prophesied by the prophets of the Old Covenant and by Jesus Christ. The Holy Spirit is therefore a firm promise that was waiting to come true. This promise was fulfilled at Pentecost over a hundred and twenty people gathered, including the mother and brothers of Jesus of Nazareth.

The Holy Spirit has been a promise from God since the time of the prophets when the Israelites had difficulty honoring the Law of Moses. The man having difficulty honoring the commandments written on tablets of stone, God considered writing these commands on the very heart of the man, in order to ensure his eternal fidelity. The Holy Spirit is that promise. The Lord said by the mouth of the prophet:

> «*I will give you a new heart, and **I will put a new spirit within you**. And I will take away the stony heart out of your flesh, and I will give you a heart of flesh. And **I will put My Spirit within you** and cause you to walk in My statutes, and you shall keep My judgments and do them*» (**Ezekel 36:26-27**).

> «*But this shall be the covenant that I will cut with the house of Israel: after those days, says Jehovah, I will put My law in their inward parts, **and write it in their hearts**; and I will be their God, and they shall be My people. And they shall no more teach each man his neighbor and each man his brother, saying, know Jehovah; for they shall all know Me, from the least of them to the greatest of them, says Jehovah. For I will forgive their iniquity, and I will remember their sins no more*» (**Jeremiah 31:33-34 / Hebrew 8:10-11**).

«*And it shall be afterward, **I will pour out My Spirit on all flesh**. And your sons and your daughters shall prophesy; your old men shall dream dreams; your young men shall see visions*» (**Joel 2:28 (3:1)**).

It is important to point out that the pouring of the Holy Spirit was initiated by Jesus Christ the Prophet promised when Moses complained of the heavy workload for his shoulders, as it is written:

«*Jehovah your God will raise up to you **a prophet** from the midst of you, of your brothers, **one like me**. To him you shall listen, according to all that you desired of Jehovah your God in Horeb in the day of the assembly, saying: let me not hear again the voice of Jehovah my God, neither let me see this great fire anymore, so that I do not die. And Jehovah said to me, they have spoken well what they have spoken. I will raise them up a **prophet from among their brothers, one like you**, and will put My words in his mouth. And he shall speak to them all that I shall command him*» (**Deuteronomy 18:15-18**).

It is this Prophet that most Jews are still waiting for until now. But for Christians, Christ has already come to save those whom He approves. He will come back a second time to judge the world. He will take this opportunity to refresh the memories of his Jewish brothers (**Zechariah 12:10**).

The solution that God brought to man, irreparably sinful and disposed to evil from his youth (**Genesis 8:21**), was to inscribe His commandments, no longer on stone tables – whose paper is the remote symbol – but in the very heart of man.

- A Law

> «*But **the law of the Spirit of life in Christ Jesus** has made me free from the law of sin and death*» **Romans 8:2**.

A law is an almost immutable device as long as it is not repealed. It is based on a consensus accepted by all. By **Romans 8:2** above, the Holy Spirit is considered a Law of life. That is, those who have the Holy Spirit are declared alive while those who do not have Him are declared dead. This is why Jesus answered one of His disciples: *Let the* (spiritual) *dead bury their* (biological) *dead*. Jesus spoke of those who had no part in His Gospel. Those who have no part in the Gospel of Christ do neither possess the Son (Christ) nor the Father. They are spiritually dead, that is, their human spirit does not harbor the Holy Spirit.

- ## A Signature

> «*In whom (Jesus) also you, hearing the word of truth, the gospel of our salvation, in whom also believing, you were **sealed with the Holy Spirit of promise**»* **Ephesians 1:13**.

The presence of the Holy Spirit in the Christian is the signature of God attesting that this Christian is the son of God. He is a disciple of Jesus Christ. He who does not have the Holy Spirit in him is not a Christian, no matter how faithful he is to church activities.

That is why every Christian, aware of this absolute truth, should make sure that he has the Holy Spirit within him. He is obtained by faith. But according to Scripture, faith is not only the assurance of substance we hope for, but also the evidence of substance promised **(Hebrews 11:1)**. Faith captures an invisible object – believing that the object (Holy Spirit) has been received – before the object becomes visible and touchable. The passage from the invisible world to the visible one rewards the faith of the Christian. Faith is therefore a process. Thus, even if at the beginning there is no evidence of the real presence of the Holy Spirit in us, little by little, the visible manifestations will testify of His real presence.

- A Person: God

> « *Then **the Spirit said to Philip**, go near and join yourself to this chariot»* **Acts 8:29**.

> «*But the **Spirit expressly says** that in the latter times some shall depart from the faith, giving heed to seducing spirits and teachings of demons»* **1 Timothy 4:1**.

> «*He who has an ear, let him hear what the **Spirit says** to the churches»* **Revelation 2:7**.

The Holy Spirit is a person

The Holy Spirit cannot be denied His personification because Jesus Christ entrusted Him with a mission to His elect: that of reminding what he had said, and leading His elect to the truth. Such a mission cannot be entrusted to an impersonal person. Jesus told His disciples that He would not leave them orphans, that He would ask the Father to send them a Comforter who will be constantly with them. This Comforter, the Holy Spirit, has the right to speak in the name of Jesus Christ. Jesus, a person, can only be represented by a person. Otherwise it would be very degrading for our glorious Lord.

According to the verses above, the Holy Spirit is a person, a person who speaks to men and women. He even convicts the world of sin, of righteousness, and of judgment (**John 16:8**). The words "*The Spirit says ...*" attest to the personification of the Holy Spirit. The Holy Spirit is not only a power, He is also a person.

The Holy Spirit is God.

«*But if the Spirit of the One who raised up Jesus from the dead dwells in you, the One who raised up Christ from the dead shall also make your mortal bodies alive by His Spirit who dwells in you*» (**Romans 8:11**).

The Holy Spirit gives life. It has never been said that the man or the angel gave life. It is God alone who gives it. In **Romans 8:11** above, it is said that it is through the Holy Spirit that God gives life to the mortal body of the Christian.

On the other hand, the presence of the Holy Spirit in the Christian brings the latter from human nature to the divine nature – see below. It was by receiving the Holy Spirit – coming as a dove – that Jesus could do the miracles He did. He said, "*But if I cast out demons **by the Spirit of God**...*" (**Matthew 12:28**).

It was not by an angel or a human spirit that Jesus could accomplish His miracles and healings.

The divine status of the Holy Spirit is seen everywhere in the Scriptures. The Holy Spirit quotes the Father and the Son (Jesus Christ) as His equal. He never says "*The Father or the Son sends me to tell you this or that ...*" like angels and prophets of the Old Covenant. The angels and the prophets always specified the one in whose name they spoke. God and His Son – Jesus Christ – are regularly represented by the Holy Spirit. The Holy Spirit is always on the same level as the Father and the Son. Just as the natural mind has the same nature as man and represents him perfectly, so the Spirit of God has the same nature as God which He perfectly represents.

At the end of the book of Revelation, after announcing the acts that Christ will put on His return, Scripture concludes with these words:

> «*And the **Spirit** and the bride say, come! And let the one hearing say, come! And let the one who is thirsty come. And he willing, let him take of the water of life freely*» (**Revelation 22:17**).

Here, Jesus Christ is represented by the Spirit in **verse 17** above. In fact, in the Old and New Testaments, God and the Lamb (Son) have been regularly paraphrased by the Spirit in their communication to men and women, showing that the Holy Spirit is God.

- A Gift

> *«Peter said to them, repent and be baptized, every one of you, in the name of Jesus Christ to remission of sins, and you shall receive **the gift of the Holy Spirit**» Acts 2:38.*

A donation is free. The Holy Spirit is therefore offered FREE of charge to anyone who asks God. Jesus exclaimed, "*If you then, being evil, know how to give good gifts to your children, **how much more shall your heavenly Father give the Holy Spirit to those who ask Him?**" (**Luke 11:13**).

Let us remember the abjection and astonishment provoked by magician Simon who wanted to acquire for money the power to transmit the Holy Spirit by laying on of hands. Peter said to this magician, "*May your silver perish with you, because you have thought that the gift of God may be purchased with money*" (**Acts 8:20**).

The Holy Spirit is the gift – free – of God who is not for sale.

- A Power

> *«But you shall receive **power, the Holy Spirit** coming upon you. And you shall be witnesses to Me both in Jerusalem and in all Judea, and in Samaria, and to the end of the earth»* **Acts 1:8**.

> *«May the God of hope fill you with all joy and peace in believing, that you may abound in hope through the **power of the Holy Spirit***» **Romans 15:13**.

> *«Now to Him who is able to do exceeding abundantly above all that we ask or think, according to the **power** that works in us»* **Ephesians 3:20**.

It takes power to resurrect a dead person. Now it was through the power of the Holy Spirit that Jesus was raised from the dead. It is indeed written:

> *«But if the Spirit of the One who raised up Jesus from the dead dwells in you, the One who raised up Christ from the dead **shall also make your mortal bodies alive by His Spirit** who dwells in you»* (**Romans 8:11**).

It is understood from this verse that the Holy Spirit, present in the Christian, gives life to the body – mortal – of the Christian. For the gift of the Holy Spirit did not abolish the consequences of sentencing Adam and his descendants to death in Eden Garden. However, the gift of the Holy Spirit gives the Christian authority and power to fulfill the will and justice of God. It is the presence of the Holy Spirit in man who makes him pass from human nature to the divine nature, according to the Scriptures – see below. It is the Holy Spirit who is the transforming power.

- A Warrior

> *«And take the helmet of salvation, and the **sword of the Spirit**, which is the word of God»* **Ephesians 6:17**.

The Spirit has a sword which is the Word of God, the Scripture. We all know that a warrior owns a weapon. The Holy Spirit is therefore a warrior. The Scriptures say that the Word of God is a sword. Note the image that Scripture gives of Jesus Christ in the Revelation of John:

> *«His head and hair were white like wool, as white as snow. And His eyes were like a flame of fire. And His feet were like burnished brass having been fired in a furnace. And His voice was like the sound of many waters. And He had seven stars in His right hand, and **out of His***

> *mouth went a **sharp two-edged sword**. And His face was like the sun shining in its strength»* **(Revelation 1:14-16)**.

Today, Jesus' tongue in His mouth is a ***sharp two-edged sword***. And as Jesus is the incarnate Word of God (**John 1:1**), this confirms that the Scripture is a sword in the hands of the Holy Spirit to whom Jesus entrusted the mission of representing Him among Christians.

- The Lord's Envoy to earth

> *«But the Comforter, the Holy Spirit **whom the Father will send in My name**, He shall teach you all things and bring all things to your remembrance, whatever I have said to you»* **John 14:26**.

Just as the Father sent Jesus Christ, Jesus Christ also sent the Holy Spirit. The Holy Spirit is therefore a continuation of the work started by Jesus Christ on earth, which lasted three years.

The Holy Spirit is the Messiah of God on the earth right now, waiting for the promised return of Jesus Christ.

- The only fellowship with the Father, the Son and other Christians

> « *If anyone has not the Spirit of Christ, he is none of His*» **Romans 8:9**.

> «*Everyone who denies the Son neither has the Father. The one confessing the Son also has the Father*» **1 John 2:23**.

> «*And truly **our fellowship is with the Father and with His son Jesus Christ***» **1 John 1:3**.

> «*But if we walk in the light, as He (God) is in the light, **we have fellowship with one another**, and the blood of Jesus Christ His Son cleanses us from all sin*» **1 John 1:7**.

There are many forms of fellowship in the visible world. We will mention some of them:

By physical contact. It is the most known fellowship among men and women. For example: two hands tightening, the embrace between two people, a pull with several arms.

By convergence of mind. Two people who debate and find common ground.

By convergence of feelings. Two people who love each other

By convergence of culture. Two people who share the same music and passion.

By other convergences. Two people living in the same house, the same neighborhood, the same town, the same city, the same country, the same continent, etc.

The world is customary of all these forms of fellowship. On the other hand, only those who possess the Spirit of Christ are part of His fold and can commune with Him. Without the Holy Spirit, any form of fellowship is carnal. The different fellowships to which the world is accustomed are carnal. Christians should avoid making much of it in the sheepfold of the Lord.

Attention, it is not forbidden for a Christian to be in communion with the world by the ways described above. The Christian, however, should be instructed that only fellowship in the Spirit has spiritual value. What is flesh is flesh. What is Spirit is Spirit. The Christian being born of water and Spirit, he now cultivates his sanctification by walking in the Spirit with all his heart. The Christian cannot commune with the world in the Spirit of Jesus.

The Christian lives in the visible and touchable world. He is therefore strongly tempted to walk by sight and appearance like the world. And that's where the seduction lies. The Christian is seduced when he relies strongly on the physical gatherings and pleasing words of those he sees. The physical persons we see may well hide a devious and perverse mind. Being in front of a perverse person does not make him holy. In the same way Scripture invites us to be wary of the pleasant words of a perverse person.

God therefore recommends a holy approach, free from the tendencies of the flesh that are those of the world: if the Christian walks in the light as God is in the light, then he is in fellowship with the other Christians – in the Spirit of course. The blood of Jesus Christ cleanses him from all sin (**1 John 1:6-7**).

TO BE BORN OF THE SPIRIT: THE YEAR ONE OF THE CHRISTIAN LIFE

Receiving the Holy Sprit

If one comes into the world by the operation of the blood, by the will of the flesh or by the will of the man, on the other hand, one enters the sheepfold of Christ – new birth – by the operation of the Holy Spirit. Whoever receives the Holy Spirit is definitely the son of God the Father, heir of God and joint-heir with Christ.

Many verses of the Scripture state that whoever does not have the Spirit of Christ does not belong to Him. Whoever does not have the Spirit of Christ has neither the Son nor the Father.

- Who can receive the gift of the Holy Spirit?

> «*Then Peter said to them, repent and be baptized, every one of you, in the name of Jesus Christ to remission of sins,* **and you shall receive the gift of the Holy Spirit**» **Acts 2:38**.

Anyone who, first of all, repents of his former life by believing that Jesus Christ is the Son of God, the expiatory Lamb, and secondly, is baptized with water, may receive the gift of the Holy Spirit as seal of his belonging to Christ.

- How does one receive the baptism/gift of the Holy Spirit?

> *«I (John the Baptist) indeed baptize you with water to repentance. But He who comes after me is mightier than I, whose sandals I am not worthy to carry.* ***He shall baptize you with the Holy Spirit*** *and with fire»* **Matthew 3:11**.

> *«In the fulfilling of the day of Pentecost, they were all with one accord in one place. And suddenly a sound came out of the heaven as borne along by the rushing of a mighty wind, and it filled all the house where they were sitting. And tongues as of fire appeared to them, being distributed; and it sat upon each of them.* ***And they were all filled of the Holy Spirit, and began to speak in other languages, as the spirit gave them utterance»*** **Acts 2:1-4**.

> *«Then Peter said to them, repent and be baptized, every one of you, in the name of Jesus Christ to remission of sins,* ***and you shall receive the gift of the Holy Spirit»*** **Acts 2:38**.

Basic Note: To receive the baptism with the Holy Spirit, it is absolutely necessary to be already baptized with water in accordance with the Scripture. However, it has sometimes happened to receive the baptism with the Holy Spirit before that with water (see Cornelius and his family / **Acts 10:44-48**).

The first common denominator of all the above writings is that if Christians baptize with water, Christ alone baptizes with the Holy Spirit. The second common denominator is that if the water, the baptizer and the Christian are present at the baptism with water, no special presence is required at the baptism with the Holy Spirit. The third remark is that during the baptism with the Holy Spirit, extraordinary manifestations may occur without any of these manifestations always having to be present to attest to the reality of the baptism of the Holy Spirit – *as the Spirit gave them utterance*. In the case of Pentecost, the disciples received several types of languages, not one in particular.

«Then Apostles Peter and John laid their hands on them, and they received the Holy Spirit» (**Acts 8:17**).

> *«And as Paul laid his hands on them, the Holy Spirit came on them, and they spoke with tongues and prophesied»* (**Acts 19:6**).

These verses of Scripture attest that the Holy Spirit can be received by the laying on of the hands of the apostles – which was not the case at Pentecost. During the experience, some may speak in tongues or prophesy or manifest something else:

> *«And God set some in the Church, firstly, apostles; secondly, prophets; thirdly, teachers, then works of power, then gifts of healings, helps, governments, kinds of languages. **Are all apostles? Are all prophets? Are all teachers? Are all workers of power? Do all have gifts of healings? Do all speak languages? Do all interpret?»*** (**1 Corinthians 12:28-30**).

He who has received the Holy Spirit knows that he has received Him because of the extraordinary manifestation that accompanied his baptism. The Lord hates that His Christians argue on any particular gift that only they MUST receive at the baptism with the Holy Spirit. At the end of the questions of **1 Corinthians 12:30** above, we understand that every Christian baptized with the Holy Spirit can be (i) an apostle without being a prophet (ii) a prophet without being a doctor (iii) a doctor without performing miracles (iv) a miracle maker without healing (v) a healer without speaking in tongues (vi) a speaker in tongues without interpreting them (vii) an interpreter of tongues without governing (viii) a governor without being a helper. Anyone who supports the opposite, who insists on specific signs that MUST be present, surrenders to visions and is puffed up with pride. He does not have to spread information under the pretext that great servants of God support them. God does not consider anyone opposing what He says explicitly in His holy Word. No He doesn't.

- **The baptism of the Holy Spirit does not dispense of baptism with water**

> «*While Peter was still speaking these words, the Holy Spirit fell on all those hearing the word. And those of the circumcision, who believed (as many as came with Peter), were astonished because the gift of the Holy Spirit was poured out on the nations also. For they heard them speak with tongues and magnify god. Then Peter answered,* **can anyone forbid water that these, who have received the Holy Ghost as well as we, should not be baptized?**» **Acts 10:44-48**.

This quotation from the Scriptures is fundamental because it was the first time that pagans – other than the biological descendants of Abraham and of Isaac and of Jacob – were receiving the gift of the Holy Spirit, without having been previously baptized with water as usual. Was it necessary to dispense with water baptism because they had received the Holy Spirit? The answer of Apostle Peter clears the question: No one is exempt from baptism with water even though he is baptized with the Holy Spirit first.

So anyone who has been baptized with the Holy Spirit, before the baptism with water, must be baptized with water.

- **May the Christian make sure that the Holy Spirit dwells in him**

> «*But if anyone has not the Spirit of Christ, he is none of His*» **Romans 8:9**.

Make no mistake, he who does not have the Holy Spirit, the Spirit of Christ, does not belong to Him. The good news for every Christian is that the Holy Spirit has been freely promised to those who ask for It: "*God does not give the Spirit by measure*" (**John 3:34**). The Christian must therefore make sure that he has the Holy Spirit dwelling in him. The work of the Holy Spirit in the Christian is real and detectable by him. The Christian must have no doubt about the presence and work of the Holy Spirit in him. If in doubt, he must ask the Lord for confirmation, but secretly – as explained later. The Lord will not be offended by his request.

The reality is that there are people who, calling themselves Christians, do not have the Holy Spirit in them (**Acts 19:2-6**). It is difficult to identify such Christians because Scripture states that only Jesus Christ knows those who belong to Him (**2 Timothy 2:19**). Any other teaching is inappropriate. The Lord has not entrusted anyone to check on who has the Holy Spirit and who doesn't. If such a checking were to be put in place, this drift would lead the Church to confusion. The devil could use it to destroy many true Christians, portraying them as pagans while they are saints. If the Pharisees have said of Jesus that he was of Satan (**Matthew 12:24**), will the faithful of the devil – disguised as angels of light in the churches – not defame true Christians to sow confusion? According to **Acts 19:2-6** above, Apostle Paul acts with caution in asking his listeners whether *they received the Holy Spirit when they believed.* He never deliberately declared that these people did not have the Holy Spirit. It was after a real investigation, helped by the same people, that he came to the conclusion that they had not received the Holy Spirit. Then he solved the problem immediately.

Precision. When Apostle John asks *to test the spirits to know if they are of God* (**1 John 4:1**), he invites to be wary of those who make unfounded or erroneous remarks, while pretending to be Christians, in the only purpose of fooling the sheep of the Lord. Wolves disguised as sheep have several times looted the sheepfold of the Lord in the history of the Church from the first century to the present day. A certain vigilance could have avoided many of these dramas. For example, at the time of John's warning, some argued that Christ never came in the flesh. This is why, following the verse calling for vigilance, Apostle John declares:

> *«By this you know the Spirit of God: every spirit that confesses that **Jesus Christ has come in the flesh** is of God; and every spirit that does not confess that Jesus Christ has come in the flesh is not of God. And this is the antichrist you heard is coming, and even now is already in the world»* (**1 John 4:2-3**).

By this warning, Apostle John prevented the adepts of this false doctrine from spreading it in the Church. It can be said that the apostle's warning bore fruit because very few people profess this heresy today.

Once again, it is in the interest of the Christian to ensure that he has the Holy Spirit, the Spirit of truth, the Spirit of Christ within him. Having the Holy Spirit in oneself is the beginning of a prosperous Christian life. Otherwise, this person deceives himself. That he does not say to himself that his participation in Church's activities will give him the epithet of a Christian in front of the Lord. We are Christians in front of the Lord and not in front of men and women attending a church. We do not flatter the Lord. We do not buy it with the activities – sacrifices. If a Christian, in doubt, puts the question to the Lord, the Lord will enlighten him because He loves the truth. Without the Holy Spirit, no man has any inheritance in the kingdom of heaven. Any business checking the presence of the Holy Spirit in one self must be SECRET. We insist on SECRET. The Christian must not reveal his doubt to anyone, to other Christians of the Church, or even to pastors because he does not know who is really who. Let him bring this question secretly before the Lord, and God who sees in secret will enlighten him. The Christian will have no doubt about the Lord's response. The Lord will watch over it. A quick check is to pray to the Lord to reveal how He sees us. He will give an image of our self as He sees it. I have known Christians who have gone through this process. Believe me, the results were uplifting. Above all, do not panic if the answer seems negative. It is not forbidden for doubts to burst into the life of a Christian. The prophet John the Baptist had doubts. Even if his example is not flattering, it indicates that at some point, doubt may appear. Apostle Paul also had doubts (**2 Corinthians 1:8-9**). Do not panic, the Lord will answer. He answered John the Baptist. He answered Paul (**v9**). He will answer also those who have doubts. It is better to start on the right foot, because we will not regret it. If ever the Christian realizes that he does not have the Holy Spirit, first he praises the Lord for revealing his true spiritual state. Repent before the Lord – even publicly if the sin in which he is entangled deserves repentance before men and women. May he sincerely ask God the Holy Spirit and he will see God respond to him with success. The Lord knows right now that he is dealing with a definitively repentant sinner. May he ask without hesitation, because Christ sincerely desires to give his Spirit to the men and women he approves. The Lord will never compromise on this issue. He will give His Spirit to anyone who sincerely asks Him – *how much more will the heavenly Father* **give the Holy Spirit to those who ask Him** (**Luke 11:13**). The purpose of this warning is not to scare, but to build on solid foundations for the good of the Christian.

- What are the gifts of the Holy Spirit received by Christians for?

> *«But to each one is given the showing forth of the Spirit **to our profit**. For through the Spirit is given to one a word of wisdom; and to another a word of knowledge, according to the same Spirit; and to another faith by the same Spirit; and to another the gifts of healing by the same Spirit; and to another workings of powers, to another prophecy; and to another discerning of spirits; and to another kinds of tongues; and to another the interpretation of tongues. But the one and the same Spirit works all these things, **distributing separately to each one as He desires»** 1 Corinthians 12:7-11.*

1 Corinthians 12 is clearly the most explicit Bible chapter on the diversification and scope of the gifts of the Spirit that Christians receive: they aim at the **common good**. They are distributed among Christians, **to each one in particular according to the will of the Holy Spirit alone**; without following a special gift, but many: prophecy, apostolate, evangelization, languages, interpretation of languages, healings, miracles, etc. It seems appropriate that for members to care for each other, the granted gifts should be different from one Christian to another. Thus, the prophet among Christian will benefit from the healing gift from the healer, and vis-versa.

The dependence of Christians on one another is a factor of diversification of gifts in the Church, so that one Christian does not rise above others, that he estimates the others above him according to that it is written, *He who is exalted will be put low, and he that is low will be exalted.*

Gifts are not for showing or selling in the church. They serve for the common edification in humility.

The temple of the Holy Spirit above the temple of Moses

«Do you not know that your body is a temple of the Holy Spirit in you, whom you have of God?» **1 Corinthians 6:19**.

*«There are priests who serve the example and shadow of heavenly things, as Moses was warned of God **when he was about to make the tabernacle**. For, He says 'See that you make all things according to the pattern shown to you in the mountain'»* **Hebrews 8:5**.

As stated in **Hebrews 8:5** above, Moses was charged by the Almighty God to build a temple following the pattern presented to him in a vision. The temple thus built was inaugurated by the blood of the animals because any testament starts with the blood. It is necessary that the death of the testator be confirmed for a will to come into execution.

Many passages of the Old Testament evoke the epic of the temple of Moses over the centuries and generations. Two elements will hold our attention: the prestige of the temple of Moses and its relation to the temple of the New Testament inaugurated by the blood of the Lamb – Jesus Christ.

• The temple of Moses was dreaded by all

The Scripture testifies that the temple of Moses, especially the ark of the covenant, was particularly dreaded. According to the Law of Moses, during wars, the troops of Israel had to go to campaign with the ark of the covenant carried by the Levitical priests. This ark symbolized the presence of God among Israel soldiers and was supposed to give them victory over their enemies. So the enemies of Israel were paralyzed at the appearance of this ark.

Even the Israelites could not approach the ark at will for fear of losing their lives. Moses thus warned the Israelites against the disappearance of the Qehathites family in charge of transporting the ark, for fear of seeing them disappear from Israel people (**Numbers 4:15, 17-20**).

In peacetime, the ark resided in the most holy place west of the tabernacle. According to the Law of Moses, only the high priest could approach it once a year at the national forgiveness ceremony.

It will be remembered that a servant of King David died trying to prevent the ark from falling. This servant did not belong to the tribe of Levi – Qehath clan – the one responsible for logistics in the most holy place. Hence the divine sanction.

The temple of Moses was therefore very scary to the Israelites themselves as well as to the people around them.

- ## The temple of Moses was only a cult of the angels

It is an extremely precious truth revealed to Apostle Paul. What does Paul say about the Law of Moses and the Gospel of Jesus Christ?

> «***The Law** was added because of transgressions, until the seed should come to those to whom it had been promised, **being ordained through angels** in the mediator's*

> *hand (Moses). But the mediator is not a mediator of one, but **God is one**»* (**Galatians 3:19-20**).

Clearly and unequivocally, Apostle Paul teaches us that despite the terror inspired by the temple of Moses and his ark, all this was only a worship of angels. These are the angels that appeared to Moses above the ark (***being ordained through angels***). It was the angels who were a pillar of fire at night and a pillar of smoke at day during the forty years pilgrimage of the Israelite people in the desert.

Therefore, God never appeared in person in the temple of Moses. One might well have guessed it because God told King Solomon, when definitively building the temple on a fixed soil, that no capped building could contain Him, God.

Regarding this cult of the angels, Apostle Paul adds:

> *«Which things are being allegorized; for these are the two covenants, one indeed from Mount Sinai bringing forth to slavery, which is Hagar. For **Hagar is Mount Sinai in Arabia**, and answers to Jerusalem which now is, and is in slavery with her children. **But the Jerusalem from above is free, who is the mother of us all**. (...) Then, brothers, we are not children of a*

*slave-woman, but of the free woman (**Sarah**)»*
(Galatians 4:24-26;31).

By these words the apostle explains that the laws of Mount Sinai were intended to keep the Israelites in slavery so that they do not reach the justice of God without today Christians. That is, the law and the Levitical priesthood were only meant to keep the Israelites in disobedience, pending the revelation of Jesus Christ, heir of Abraham, whose crucifixion at Golgotha gives to all Jews and non-Jews access to the justice by faith.

The Gospel was transmitted, not by angels – like the Law of Moses – but by Jesus Christ directly to men and women. Being God, Jesus Christ did not need a mediator because He was visible and audible to humans. He did not need angels to talk to men and women through a mediator. We can also say that the Lord Jesus is His own mediator. The angels of God needed a mediator, in the person of Moses, because they were numerous and of extraordinary appearance. We remember that their appearance on Mount Sinai was so frightening that the Israelites begged Moses to go and receive for their sake the commandments of God **(Deuteronomy 18:16)**. Moreover, it was not the same angels who intervened from one occasion to another at time of the Old Covenant.

This is the crucial point of this chapter: The temple of Moses was actually home to angels in the service of God. Although they were called 'angels of God', they were only angels. No matter how extraordinary he looks like, an angel remains an angel, not God. But Jesus is superior to angels according to the Scripture: "***Being made so much better than the angels***, *as He (Jesus) has by inheritance obtained a **more excellent name than they**"* (**Hebrews 1:4**).

God had never lived in person in a stone temple built by the hands of men, as He now dwells in Spirit in the Christian, making the latter the temple of the Holy Spirit.

- ## The Temple of the Holy Spirit above the temple of Moses

> «*Now the sum of the things which we have spoken is this: we have such a High Priest (Jesus Christ), who has sat down on the right of the Throne of the Majesty in heaven, a Minister of the sanctuary and of the true tabernacle, which the Lord pitched, and not man*» **Hebrews 8:1-2**.

Unlike the temple of Moses, the temple of the Holy Spirit – Christian – is not of human origin because the Christian is now born of God (of water and of Spirit). Even though the human spirit is transmitted biologically, the Holy Spirit, lodged in the human spirit, is not transmitted biologically. The Holy Spirit dwells in the human spirit, which is the spiritual heart (breath of God) of man at his creation. As the Holy Spirit is transmitted to men and women by God, not by blood, the Christian is no longer considered a human creation. The Christian is now part of the kingdom of heaven, the New Creation of God (**Colossians 1:15**). As a temple of the Holy Spirit, the Christian is no more a human construction like the temple of Moses.

By dwelling in the human spirit of the regenerated Christian, the Holy Spirit makes of the latter a temple superior to that of Moses at least in holiness, no less. Indeed, a place inhabited by God is holier than the place inhabited by an angel, even if he is the angel of the Lord. The Holy Spirit, true God, is now living in the Christian who as a result, becomes more important than the temple of Moses. Surprising but true.

The Christian must therefore become aware of his holiness related to the presence of the Holy Spirit in him. If the temple of Moses, built by the hands of men, was so glorious as to bring terror to the neighbors of Israel, how much more should the Christian pay attention to the presence of the Holy Spirit in him? He should adopt an irreproachable body and mind hygiene, and stop murmuring. Apostle Paul recalled what happened to the Israelites who irritated God in the desert. They perished as it is written:

> «*Nor let us commit fornication, as some of them fornicated, and twenty-three thousand fell in one day. Nor let us tempt Christ, as some of them also tempted Him and were destroyed by serpents*» (**1 Corinthians 10:8-9**).

Given the wrath of God to those who violated the worship of angels, what will happen to those who violate the worship of the Holy Spirit incarnated by His presence in the Christian? Speaking of the above sanctions, the apostle Paul affirmed:

> *«All these things happened to them as examples; and it is written **for our warning** on whom the ends of the world have come»* (**1 Corinthians 10:11**).

> *«See that you do not refuse him who speaks (angel through Moses). For if they did not escape, those who refused him that spoke on earth, much more we shall not escape if we turn away from Him (Jesus Christ) who speaks from heaven (through the Holy Spirit)»* (**Hebrews 12:25**).

The apostle warns of the more terrifying punishment for those who reject God and His perfect priesthood, knowing that those who refused to listen to Moses and his shadow priesthood were already under severe punishment.

Let us take sanctification seriously, as Apostle Paul recommended. Let us watch over this temple of the Holy Spirit that we are with fear and trembling. For according to the Scripture, the ministry of the Spirit is more glorious than the ministry of the letter engraved on the tables of Mount Sinai, at the heart of the Levitical priesthood:

> *«But if the ministry of death, **having been engraved in letters in stone was with glory (...) shall not the ministry of the Spirit be with more glory?*»** (**2 Corinthians 3:7-8**).

The temple of the Holy Spirit – Christian – is therefore more glorious than the temple of Moses. The Christian should therefore watch over his *sanctification without which he will not see the Lord God.* As much as the ark of the covenant – part of the temple of Moses – ensured the troops of Israel victory over their enemies, so long as the Israelites obeyed the commandments of God, so much the Christian, temple of the Holy Spirit, will have the victory over his enemies if he takes his sanctification seriously.

- ### The real form of God's temple in heaven

Apostle John made a surprising discovery by exploring the temple of God in the heavenly Jerusalem, the holy city adorned for the wedding of the Lamb. He declared:

> *«I saw no temple in it (heavenly Jerusalem), for the Lord God Almighty is its temple, even the Lamb»* (**Revelation 21:22**).

Surprising! God is the temple of the heavenly Jerusalem as well as the Lamb. This confirms what Jesus said to His hearers: *Destroy this temple and in three days I will raise it up.* Of course, He spoke of the temple of His body as the Scriptures specify (**John 2:19-21**).

In declaring "*I saw no temple in it (heavenly Jerusalem)*" Apostle John admits that there was no figure, no geometrical form, or object having any connection with the temple of God. There was therefore neither candlestick nor altar of perfumes nor bronze vat for ablutions, nor altar of sacrifices nor grate to recover the braziers. The true temple of God has nothing to do with a stone building or a geometric building in a given place called 'holy place'. In particular, the temple of God cannot have a roof because it is to accept that the roof is superior to God. As the temple of Moses had a roof, it is easy to understand that God Himself never appeared there. These are the angels of God who appeared to Moses as Scripture states, hence the importance of Moses as mediator between these angels and the Israelites (**Galatians 3:19-20**). Long before Moses, no one had celebrated God in a covered place. The temples were always open. The remains of ancient civilizations still have open temples, sometimes fenced, but still open.

The reality is that the temple of God is none other than the presence of God. May God appear for a short time or a long time, the temple of God is and remains His presence. Where God is, there is His temple. The temple of the heavenly Jerusalem is God and the Lamb because God dwells there with the Lamb. God being present in the Christian by His Holy Spirit, whoever deals with the Christian is dealing with the true temple of God. Does this mean that one must have a reverential posture in front of the Christian? Reverential postures have always been used by men and women in the holy places or in front of higher authorities. It's idolatry. And pagans are fond of it because they do not know God. There is no need for a reverential posture in front of a Christian. It is unfortunate that many Christians are ignorant of this truth. However, kneeling to God is a pleasant and recommended posture of pray. One cannot kneel in front of a Christian to pray because the prayer is addressed to God, not to the Christian.

The true temple of God does not have any geometrical form. The temple of God is the presence of God. To illustrate the temple of God is to illustrate the presence of God. God let humans do it when it was difficult for them to grasp this fundamental truth. The truth remains that the temple of God is His presence.

It is therefore stubbornness to wait until the temple of Moses is rebuilt. Those who say that this temple will be rebuilt are in error because the true priesthood is that of Jesus Christ, which was made by God High Priest for eternity according to Melchizedek's class. Jesus indeed inaugurated by His own blood a perfect temple not built by the hands of men. God can no longer accept a temple of stones while the perfect temple, inaugurated by the blood of the Lamb, already exists!

The temple built by Moses was a symbol awaiting the One who would build the perfect temple with better dispositions. The temple of Moses was made of stone, inaugurated by the blood of animals, and directed by mortal and sinful Levitical priests. But the temple of God in heaven is God Himself and the Lamb. It was inaugurated by the blood of Jesus of Nazareth, a blood that *speaks better than that of animals and Abel the righteous.* This temple is led by a perfect High Priest, Jesus Christ, immaculate, stainless, immortal.

Biological death, death of the spirit, death of hell

«Jehovah God commanded the man, saying, you may freely eat of every tree in the garden, but you shall not eat of the tree of knowledge of good and evil. For in the day that you eat of it you shall surely die» **Genesis 2:16-17.**

«All the days that Adam lived were nine hundred and thirty years. And he died» **Genesis 5:5.**

«But Jesus said to him, follow me, and let the dead bury their dead» **Matthew 8:22.**

*«And death and hell were cast into the lake of fire. **This is the second death»** Revelation 20:14.*

Important notice: the Spirit with capital 'S' cannot die because He is God. But the spirit of man with small 's' can die, for the spirit of man is not God; it's a creature unlike the Holy Spirit.

There is no doubt that death does not have the same meaning when one goes through the Scriptures. Let say that there is death and death. The four passages above state it. When the Scripture claims that Adam died at nine hundred and thirty years (**Genesis 5:5**), it is the biological death of the ancestor of humans: a state of total inertia where there is no activity, neither light nor motion.

When Jesus asks to let the dead bury their dead, we understand that we are dealing with two types of 'death'. The dead person to be buried is biologically dead – corpse. What about the dead that buries the corpse? How can a dead bury another dead? Are we not used to seeing the alive bury the dead? However **Matthew 8:22** states that the dead can also bury a dead, and the Scripture doesn't lie. Hence the obvious question: Who is the dead who buries the biologically dead? The one who buries is not biologically dead because biological death is a state of total inertia, without activity. This is inevitably another form of death that we will discover later.

Finally, Scripture declares that the lake of fire, hell, is the second death (**Revelation 20:14**), a definitive death to which those who have accepted Christ as their Savior and Lord will escape. The Scripture says: "*Blessed and holy is he who has part in the first resurrection. **The second death has no authority over these**, but they will be priests of God and of Christ, and will reign with Him a thousand years*" (**Revelation 20:6**).

- Biological and physical death

We will not spend time on this chapter because it is the most usual death of humans. When we lose our loved ones, we say that they are biologically dead. Even Jesus died biologically on the cross where He was hanged. His body was buried. Biological or physical death leads to burial and dust.

Let us note that the biological death remains a sanction pronounced by God on Adam and his descendants the humans. Men and women all die in Adam. That is to say, biological death is only the distant consequence of the death sentence pronounced by God on our first ancestors. Indeed, after Adam's disobedience by eating of the tree of knowledge of good and evil he was forbidden to consume, God said to him: "*In the sweat of your face you shall eat bread until you return to the ground, for out of it you were taken.* ***For dust you are, and to dust you shall return***"(**Genesis 3:19**).

In taking a human form, Jesus did not escape this course because he came to save Adam's descendants. To do this, He had to go through all stages of human life, from birth to death. He went through this process successfully; then "*God has highly exalted Him, and has given Him a name which is above every name, that at the name of Jesus every knee should bow, of heavenly ones, and of earthly ones, and of ones under the earth; and that every tongue should confess that Jesus Christ is Lord, to the glory of God the Father*" (**Philippians 2:9-11**).

Biological death is therefore a state of corpse, of total inertia, without activity, light, or shade of variation. The result is buried underground.

- Death of the spirit – Spiritual death

We have defined the human spirit as residing around the biological heart of man. The human spirit is also called spiritual heart. It is the spiritual heart that receives the Holy Spirit at the regeneration of the Christian. The reason is that in the beginning, God blew into the nostrils of the man before the biological heart of him began to beat (**Genesis 2:7**). Since then, the heart of man beats continuously. During natural reproduction by man and woman, the fetus' heart beats continuously and stops only at biological death. Originally, man is an inert dust. It is from the breath of God in his nostrils that a man became a living being. This life is caused by the circulation of blood in his veins, a blood propelled into the human tissue by the biological heart. It is this original breath of God that has resulted into the (human) spirit, and it resides around the biological beating heart. The human spirit was originally intended only to make man alive. He was not holy as the Holy Spirit, yet he was innocent, that is, without sin or condemnation. The Holy Spirit cannot sin. But the human spirit can sin even if, in the beginning, he was innocent. It is by disobeying God that man has lost his innocence to become a recidivist sinner. When we talk about circumcision of the heart – contrary to biological circumcision in removing the foreskin – we mean regeneration of the spiritual heart. One does not circumcise the biological heart, but one circumcises the spiritual heart or human spirit. For a Christian, the human spirit – spiritual heart – is circumcised when enlivened by the Holy Spirit.

God had promised regeneration – circumcision – of the spiritual heart through the prophet. It is indeed written:

> *«But this shall be the covenant that I will cut with the house of Israel: after those days, says Jehovah, I will put My law in their inward parts, and **write it in their hearts**; and I will be their God, and they shall be My people»* **(Jeremiah 31:33).**

> ***«I will give you a new heart, and I will put a new spirit within you»* (Ezekiel 36:26)**.

We understand from the above verses that the regenerative operations of the born-again Christian take place in his spiritual heart or human spirit. It is in the human spirit (spiritual heart) of man that comes and dwells the Holy Spirit for regeneration. It is said of him who receives the Holy Spirit thus, that he is a Christian, a saint, a disciple of Jesus Christ.

How then does the human spirit die? How does the spiritual heart die? This is an excellent question that requires an unequivocal answer. **The human spirit dies when it is separated from God or when it leaves the presence of God**. Every death, in the absolute, means: **Separated from God**. Whoever is separated from God is simply dead. But to say simply, every person separated from God is *spiritually* dead. This is what Jesus insinuated by saying to *let the (spiritual) dead bury their (biological) dead.*

Whoever is separated from God is dead. Even if one lives biologically or clinically, one is spiritually dead when he is separated from God.

Having been expelled from Eden Garden, a heavenly place, Adam and Eve were spiritually dead. Their spiritual heart was separated from God. Their inner eyes – another appellation of the spiritual heart – could no longer grasp God's presence. Although

Adam died biologically aged nine hundred and thirty years, his spiritual death had already been pronounced when he was expelled from Eden Garden.

> Let us understand that death, in the absolute, is the separation from God. Whoever is separated from God is dead.

One can thus have cases where one lives biologically while being spiritually dead: this is the case of Adam who was declared dead before his biological death. It is also the case of his pagan descendants who do not believe that Jesus Christ is the Son of God, the atoning Lamb who takes away the sin of the world. This is still the case of the gravedigger of **Matthew 8:22**. One can also be biologically dead while being spiritually alive: this is the case of saints who are no longer of this world. They live with God in paradise where they perfect their sanctification. The Scripture indeed speaks of the *spirits of just men made perfect* (**Hebrews 12:23**). Jesus, in response to the Sadducees who challenged the resurrection of the dead, affirmed that God was the Father of Abraham, Isaac, and Jacob. One way to say that despite being biologically dead, these three patriarchs were spiritually alive (**Matthew 22:32-33**).

As one goes through the scriptures, it is easy to conclude that most of all God cares about the health of the human spirit that He first breathed into the nostrils of man. If man is separated from God, then his human spirit is dead. In this case, the man is dead whether he is biologically alive or dead. When the spirit is dead, it does not matter to God that you live biologically. God is so worried that He sent His only begotten Son, Jesus of Nazareth, as a means of expiation and reconciliation of man with Him. Scripture says that:

> «*God was in Christ **reconciling the world to Himself**, not imputing their trespasses to them, and putting the word of reconciliation in us*» (**2 Corinthians 5:19**).

Man's reconciliation with God takes place when he receives the Holy Spirit in his spirit. It is said of this man that he is regenerated, born again, a Christian, a saint, a disciple of Jesus Christ, a heart-circumcised. While one who does not believe is already judged. He is (spiritually) dead even though he lives biologically. The soul of this person is in danger because he risks to be thrown into hell – the second death – at the end of time, when God will judge the living and the dead.

Based on the foregoing, we understand that Satan and his angels are spiritually dead because they have definitely and irreversibly left the presence of God. They are destined for hell, the second death.

- ## Death of the hell – Second death

God reserved hell for Satan and the angels who followed him in rebellion. They are commonly called demons. When they left God's presence, they died spiritually. Scripture gives them unflattering names. Worse still, God has not foreseen remission for these fallen angels. There is no longer any reconciliation for them. Their sins are inexpiable, Jesus did not come to save the fallen angels, otherwise Jesus would have taken both human and angel form during His lifetime on earth. Scripture attests explicitly, unequivocally, that hell was reserved for Satan and his angels. In a parable, Jesus said:

> *«Then He (God) also shall say to those on the left hand, depart from Me, you cursed, into **everlasting fire prepared for the devil and his angels*** (**Matthew 25:41**).

It is sad that humans go into the hell fire reserved, originally, to Satan and his angels. This is the reality of Scriptures. Those who have not repented of their sins, those who have trampled on the blood of Jesus Christ will go to hell, it is the second death.

> *«And death and hell were cast into the lake of fire. **This is the second death*** (**Revelation 20:14**).

Glory to God: Christians who will stand firm and persevere until the end will have the right to the resurrection of the just. They will reign with Christ. The second death, hell, will have no effect on them as it is written:

> «*Blessed and holy is he who has part in the first resurrection. **The second death (hell) has no authority over these**, but they will be priests of God and of Christ, and will reign with Him a thousand years*» (**Revelation 20:6**).

TO LIVE IN THE SPIRIT

The Christian is born not of the blood, nor of the will of the flesh, nor of the will of man, but of God, of water and of the Spirit

*«But as many as received Him, He gave to them authority to become the children of God, to those who believe on His name, who were born, **not of bloods, nor of the will of the flesh, nor of the will of man**, but were born of God»* **John 1:12-13**.

*«Truly, truly, I say to you, unless a man is born of **water and the Spirit**, he cannot enter into the kingdom of God»* **John 3:5**.

We cannot afford to underestimate the four gospels in relation to the Acts of the Apostles on the pretext that the Gospels predate Pentecost. Even though some passages of the gospels have not been recalled by the apostles, their spiritual reality remains. If Jesus, of His time, reminded David of the Old Testament, should we not recall His actions from the four Gospels? Jesus Christ is superior to the greatest apostle if any. One could even give more importance to the Gospels than to the Acts of the Apostles. Is Jesus not the greatest Prophet? At least we know that He was greater than King David whom He quoted in His messages, and whose psalms we value. Pentecost was only the trigger for the missionary work of the apostles under the guidance of the Holy Spirit. This does not detract from the gospels which are directly related to Jesus Christ. Jesus

Christ made it clear in which frame the Holy Spirit, coming after Him, would intervene: *He will teach you all things and remember all that I have told you* (**John 14:26**). Logically one can assimilate the gospel to a fundamental law and the Acts of the Apostles to the texts of application. Never has an application text gone beyond the law on which it is based.

That said, we must pay special attention to verse **John 1:13** above. It is reported that those who were given to believe in the name of Jesus, are no longer born of the blood nor of the will of the flesh, nor of the will of man. The blood, the will of the flesh and the will of man are three basic elements characterizing all those born of women. They are all born of blood. How is it that a disciple of Jesus, engendered by the operation of the blood (placenta), the will of the flesh and the will of man, can claim to be *born of God, of water and of the Spirit*? Jesus says indeed, a little further in the same chapter, "*Unless a man is **born of water and the Spirit**, he cannot enter into the kingdom of God*" (**John 3:5**). This is the mystery of the new birth – regeneration – that the Pharisee Nicodemus had difficulty understanding, since he wondered if he should return to his mother's womb to be reborn. Whoever is born again is reputed to be born of God. Whoever is born again is also born of water and the Spirit (**verses 3 and 7**).

> Born of God, born again or born of water and Spirit describe one and same reality. A reality opposed to that of the

> rest of the humans who are born of blood, of the will of the flesh and of the will of the man.

It is now up to the Christian to grasp the force of this truth and to make it his own. It is this great distinction which separates him from those of the world. The latter do not have in them the Holy Spirit whom they cannot know (**John 14:17**).

God does not ask Christians to understand or explain that. He says it's the spiritual reality of every Christian. By the way, it is not difficult to understand if we accept that whoever has the Holy Spirit of God in him is a new creature. The Spirit of God, in man, is a gift from God. An exceptional gift since it was the main target of the prophets of the Old Testament, and the angels wish to look into it (**1Peter 1:10-12**).

The natural man does not understand the things of the Spirit (**1 Corinthians 2:14**) for the simple reason that he does not have in him the Spirit of God, that Spirit God had promised to engrave in the heart of men and women (**Ezekiel 36:26-27**). The presence (or absence) of the Holy Spirit in the human establishes the border between a Christian and a pagan – spiritually dead as described above. Jesus said "*Let the (spiritual) dead bury their (biological) dead*" (**Luke 9:60**).

It is a grace of God to receive His Spirit. He who has the Spirit of Christ belongs to Christ. And he who does not have Him, does not belong to Jesus (**Romans 8:9**). He who has the Spirit of God is a new creature. He is born of God, of water and Spirit. He who does not have the Spirit of God is dead (spiritually) because he lives only by the blood, the will of the flesh and the will of man.

Every Christian must henceforth consider himself born of God, having nothing to do with the blood or the flesh – placenta. It requires the Christian to rethink his relationship with the world, because he is no longer considered as an entity of the world to make its will. He is now born of God to fulfill the righteousness of God and only He. Here we must avoid confusion and exceptions as there is no exception to this rule. There is no exception in this regard concerning biological parents. Indeed, the Lord declares, "*If anyone comes to Me and **does not hate his father and mother and wife and children and brothers and sisters, yes, and his own life also, he cannot be My disciple**"(***Luke 14:26***). The absence of exception also extends to the life of Christians. Jesus Christ demands that the Christian even gives up his own life if he wants to be His disciple. This is the challenge that awaits every Christian, and no exception is allowed.

This peculiar status of the Christian, unlike the pagan, is very well explained in the Gospel of Jesus Christ. Such an allusion is also present in the epistles of the apostles as it is written: "*Those belonging to Christ* (born again) *have crucified the flesh with its* *passions and lusts. **If we live in the Spirit** (for we are born again), let us also walk in the Spirit"* (**Galatians 5:24-25**).

Note well the term used in **Galatians 5:24**: *if we live in the Spirit*, (THEN) *let us also walk in the Spirit*. So the condition for walking in the Spirit is to be born of the Spirit. Just as the natural man lives in the flesh because born of blood, the disciple of Christ, on the other hand, lives in the Spirit because he is born of the Spirit. **It is because one is born of the flesh that one lives in the flesh. It is also because we are born of the Spirit that we live in the Spirit.** Now, as the natural man walks in the flesh, because born of this material, God requires that the Christian walk in the Spirit because he is born of the Spirit. It is by walking in the Spirit that the Christian will fulfill the righteousness of God. However, it is possible for him to walk in the flesh because of the envelope that surrounds him, that inherited from his biological parents. But God does not allow it, hence vigilance. As Christians are born of the Spirit, then they must walk in the Spirit. God requires it because those who walk in the flesh cannot please Him as it is written: *"The carnal mind is enmity against God, for it is not subject to the law of God, neither indeed can it be"* (**Romans 8:7**). The natural man cannot walk in the Spirit who is totally unknown to him. He can only follow the tendencies of the flesh because his mind is cut off from God – spiritually dead. Every human spirit, not live-quickened by the Holy Spirit, is dead. As the natural man does not have the Holy Spirit in him, he does not belong to Christ. And whoever does not belong to Christ is dead. The Christian, on the other hand, has the Holy Spirit abiding in him, that is why he lives in the Spirit, whether he likes it or not, understands it or not, accepts it or not, guarantees it or not. Therefore, on this basis, he must ABSOLUTELY **walk in the Spirit** to fulfill God's righteousness. However, it is possible for him to reconnect with the tendencies of the flesh because he remains always enclosed in a terrestrial envelope. God is against these tendencies as Apostle Paul made known

> to the Galatians who, after having walked in the Spirit, had fallen back to flesh tendencies. So the apostle reminded them that as **they were born of the Spirit**, so they had to walk in the Spirit and give up flesh tendencies. He reminded them that formerly they walked in the Spirit, and wondered at seeing them fall back into the flesh of which they were no longer indebted. He who is not born of the Spirit, cannot walk in the Spirit. But to walk in the Spirit is to show faith. He who does not walk in the Spirit, does not have faith and *without faith, we cannot please God* (**Hebrews 11:6**).

Living in the world does not allow the Christian to share the values of the world without precaution. Coexistence with the world, as recommended by Jesus Christ Himself, must be done with delicacy. It is not a question of communing with them in spirit – for their spirit is dead without God – but rather to live in their midst while waiting for the return of the Lord who will physically separate the good and the bad. Jesus asked Christians to watch and pray, to sanctify themselves by rejecting carnal tendencies, to be cautious as serpents and as simple as doves (**Matthew 10:16**). The Christian can therefore live in the middle of the world without following his tendencies.

By the Holy Spirit, Christians are saints, members of the kingdom of heaven

The real identity of the Christian is revealed through the blessings that God gives him. He who receives the gift of prophecy is a prophet. The one who receives the pastor's gift is a pastor. Whoever receives the gift of teacher is a teacher. Just like an evangelist is he who receives the gift of evangelization. **He who receives the Holy Spirit is a saint, a member of the kingdom of heaven**.

Jesus made it clear that His kingdom was not of this world. He says to the Jews of His time:

> «*You are from beneath; **I am from above**. You are of this world; **I am not of this world***» (**John 8:23**).

Jesus indicated that His presence on earth also meant that His kingdom had come down to earth:

> «*But if I cast out demons by the Spirit of God, then **the kingdom of God has come to you***» (**Matthew 12:28**).

Later, in the last prayer to His Father, Jesus declares that His disciples, called to continue His mission after Him, were not of this world even though they were allowed to live there. He says indeed:

> «*I have given them (disciples) Your word, and the world has hated them **because they are not of the world**, even as I am not of the world. **I do not pray for You to take them out of the world**, but for You to keep them from the evil. **They are not of the world**, even as I am not of the world*» (**John 17:14-16**).

Christians are no longer of the world because they now belong to a different kingdom, that of Christ: the kingdom of heaven. Christians are therefore saints. Scripture gives them this qualifier abundantly in the Acts of Apostles. Here are a few:

> «*For it has pleased those of Macedonia and Achaia to make a certain contribution **for the poor saints in Jerusalem**» (**Romans 15:26**).*

> «*Paul, an apostle of Jesus Christ by the will of God, **to the saints who are in Ephesus, and faithful in Christ Jesus**. Grace be to you, and peace from God our Father and from the Lord Jesus Christ*» (**Ephesians 1:1-2**).

In the acts and epistles of apostles, the words 'saint', 'faithful' and 'Christian' are equal. The word 'saint' is even used extensively because, in the first century of our era, the word 'Christian' was as derogatory as the word 'sect' today.

From the status of saint, member of the kingdom of heaven, everything changes for the Christian, as we shall see below.

The natural man inherits from his father: spirit, soul and body

> *«May the God of peace Himself sanctify you, and may **your whole spirit and soul and body** be preserved blamelessly at the coming of our Lord Jesus Christ»* **1 Thessalonians 5:23**.

According to Scripture, man is made up of a spirit, a soul and a body through which human nature is defined. From one generation to another, humans transmit to their descendants what they naturally possess: a body, a spirit and a soul. Since humans cannot give birth to wild animals, reptiles, fish and birds, but only to human babies, we are certain that future generations will have a body, a spirit and a soul like Adam and Eve. That's why only humans inherit humans. Never has an angel inherited a human. Never a lion, a raven, a bird naturally inherited the man.

By making the Christian His heir and joint-heir with Christ, God gives Christian the divine nature. We will further explain God's invitation to go from human nature to the divine nature.

We must take note that humans inherit humans. This is the main base of the natural heritage. To inherit the nature of man, one must be like him. One must have been begotten by him. Whoever has not been engendered by Gerome, naturally cannot inherit Gerome. If then God sees Christians as His heirs and joint-heirs with Christ, it is because **God recognizes that He has engendered them in Christ**. This is what Scripture attests:

> «*For we are His workmanship, **created in Christ Jesus** to good works, which God has before ordained that we should walk in them*» (**Ephesians 2:10**).

> «*But as many as received Him, **He gave to them authority to become the children of God**, to those who believe on His name, **who were born**, not of bloods, nor of the will of the flesh, nor of the will of man, but were born **of God***» (**John 1:12-13**).

God believes that the Christian is begotten by Him, just as men and women are begotten by their parents. **Being born of God grants divine attributes as much as being born of biological parents grants human attributes**. The Christian must not ignore this truth. He is even invited to claim it because he has received the faith for it. It is sad that Christians do not take themselves as sons whom God has begotten as much as they are aware of having biological fathers. God wants Christians to take Him seriously since the affirmation is of Him.

But the Christian inherits the Spirit of God and the divine nature

Just as a newborn baby inherits the human spirit at birth, because his parents possess a human spirit, the Christian inherits the Holy Spirit when he confesses and believes that Jesus Christ is the Expiatory Lamb offered as a ransom for the sin of humanity. From the regeneration of his spirit (new birth), the Christian inherits the Holy Spirit. Jesus says to the Pharisee Nicodemus:

> «*Unless a man is born of water and the Spirit, he cannot enter into the kingdom of God*» (**John 3:5**).

The new birth or Christendom is a matter of the Holy Spirit. Scripture affirms that *if anyone has not the Spirit of Christ, he is none of His* (**Romans 8:9**). The new birth has nothing to do with the activities carried out in the churches. Some churches even entrusted pagans with activities for the building of the body of Christ. None of these activities will give these pagans the status of Christian. For it is by being born of the Spirit that one becomes a Christian, according to the words of Jesus; and nothing else.

Hence we should not confuse on the real identity of the Christian. The Christian has the Holy Spirit in him, the Spirit of Christ, the Spirit of God, the Spirit of truth, the Comforter.

As discussed above, if God has established that the Christian is His heir and joint-heir with Christ, then the Christian inherits the nature of God, a divine nature.

The requirements of the divine nature inherited by the Christian

«Through which (glory and virtue) He has given to us exceedingly great and precious promises, so that by these you might be **partakers of the divine nature**, *having escaped the corruption that is in the world through lust»* **2 Peter 1:4**.

«But you (Christians) have not so learned Christ, if indeed you have heard Him and were taught by Him, as the truth is in Jesus. For you ought to **put off the old man** *(according to your way of living before) who is corrupt according to the deceitful lusts, and* **be renewed in the Spirit of your mind**. *And you should* **put on the new man, who according to God was created in righteousness and true holiness»** **Ephesians 4:20-24**.

> «*Therefore **put to death your members which are on the earth**: fornication, uncleanness, passion, evil desire, and covetousness which is idolatry. (...) Do not lie to one another, **having put off the old man** with his deeds and **having put on the new**, having been renewed in knowledge according to the image of Him who created him*» **Colossians 3:5,9-10.**

In ascending these Scriptures from below upward, we learn that the Christian is summoned to *put off the old man* – corrupted by the passions and lusts that were wrought there – in order to take on the new nature whose characteristic is that it is renewed according to the image of the God who created it. **Ephesians 4:24** states that it is God who created the new nature *in righteousness and true holiness*. **Verse 23** indicates that the new nature is received thanks to the *Spirit that renews the mind (intelligence)* of the Christian. Thus, we see that the presence of the Holy Spirit in the Christian aims, among other things, to establish the **holiness of God in his mind** in order to change his tendencies, and to make him pass from old human tendencies to the divine tendencies which will grow to know God in truth – through His acts of justice.

Therefore the Christian must not prevent the renewal of his intelligence by the Holy Spirit in order to modify his nature entirely. In fact, it is not a question of improving the old human nature because human is incapable of correction. It is a question of getting rid of the human nature in favor of the new divine nature inoculated by the Holy Spirit. For before the Holy Spirit came to dwell in the spirit of the Christian, the latter was managed by his unregenerate natural spirit. At regeneration, the Holy Spirit establishes His dwelling in the spirit of the Christian – *Your body is a temple of the Holy Spirit in you, whom you have of God* (**1 Corinthians 6:19**).

The Christian must not be ashamed of this renewed nature – divine – even if such an affirmation may seem surrealistic in this world. The Christian being **born of water and Spirit**, it is obvious that he will be animated by a nature other than earthly. It is a life-giving nature as it is written:

> *«If the Spirit of the One who raised up Jesus from the dead dwells in you, the One who raised up Christ from the dead **shall also make your mortal bodies alive by His Spirit who dwells in you**»* (**Romans 8:11**).

Other translation:

> *«If the Spirit of Him, who raised our Lord Jesus Messiah from the dead, dwelleth in you; He who raised our Lord Jesus Messiah from the dead, **will also vivify your dead bodies, because of His spirit that dwelleth in you**»* (**Romans 8:11/Bible Murdoch 1851**).

It is this life inoculated into the Christian that is of divine nature. Our bodies are mortal, but the life that is inoculated by the Holy Spirit is divine. It is this nature that is being renewed day by day in order to bring the Christian to the stature of Christ (**Ephesians 4:13**). We make it clear that the Holy Spirit resides in the spirit of the Christian at regeneration. It is from that human spirit that the Holy Spirit introduces the divine life into the understanding, the feelings and the will of the Christian. It is said then that this Christian has a renewed intelligence, renewed sentiments and renewed will to the glory of God the Father. This Christian therefore passes from the human nature to the divine nature although his body remains mortal.

How does the Christian go from human nature to the divine nature?

*«But you (Christians) have not so learned Christ, if indeed you have heard Him and were taught by Him, as the truth is in Jesus. For you ought to **put off the old man** (according to your way of living before) who is corrupt according to the deceitful lusts, and **be renewed in the Spirit of your mind**. And you should put on the new man, who according to God was created in righteousness and true holiness»* **Ephesians 4:20-24**.

It is evident from **Ephesians 4:20-24** that the transition from human nature to the divine nature involves a **stripping** and **renewal**. These two actions are made possible by the presence of the Holy Spirit in the Christian. Without the Spirit of Christ, it is useless to try because it is impossible for the natural man.

If the Christian does not put a heart to it, in this process of **stripping** and **renewal**, he will soon realize that his life is no different from that before the conversion. The presence of the Holy Spirit regenerates the Christian who passes from death (natural man) to life (spiritual man).

The Lord invites the Christian to the **stripping away** of the old human nature and to **renewal** in an incorruptible divine nature because His Spirit is present in the Christian. Whatever the difficulties, the Christian must trust Christ, and what he desires will come true. This is the principle of faith in Christ: *the **substance** of things hoped for, the **evidence** of things not seen* (**Hebrews 11:1**). One must first hope for what is unseen, while having the heart – the inner eyes – fixed on Christ. It is then that God will bring forth the unseen to the visible world; so the **evidence** is complete.

Once aware of the necessity of putting off the old human nature for the benefit of the new divine nature, the Christian must accept the choices of God in all the circumstances of his life. Among the tendencies that must be put off, **Colossians 3:5** mentions in particular *misconduct, impurity, passions, bad desires and greed.* There are a plethora of other tendencies that must be stripped away and that have a close or distant connection with them.

We must specify that putting off the old nature is not always easy. It is even a dry loss because, among old tendencies to put off, there are things with an appearance of virtue such as: *do not taste, do not eat, wait for a particular day, not in such a place, etc.* Some trends are even praised by local laws.

So the Christian will avoid building his life on public opinion and traditions of this world. Only the word of God will have to serve as a compass. What is forbidden by the word of God, he will have to do without it such as, in our day, homosexuality which alas is gradually tolerated in the world (**1 Corinthians 6:10, 1 Timothy 1:10, Jude 1:7**). What the word of God allows, he must accept it no matter the hostility of the world around, because *heaven and earth will pass but the word of God will not pass*. In fact all that is visible will pass. And the wise observer can already realize that Scriptures have remained unchanged while the countries have undergone many upheavals. The great countries of today – United States, France, England, Russia, Brazil, India, China, Japan – were almost unknown in antiquity where Egypt, Greece, Italy (ancient Rome), Iran (ancient Persia) held the leading roles. It will be the same in the future because it is not certain that the advanced countries of today will still be at the forefront tomorrow. It may seem crazy to say that today, as it was crazy to imagine the disappearance of the Egyptian pharaohs and Roman emperors whose rule lasted for centuries. But what has not changed and will never change is the word of God, *the sword of the Spirit*. The Word of God has withstood earthquakes, floods, wars, cultural, civilizational, social and political upheavals, as well as weather and catastrophes of all kinds. Sometimes it was not available, but always, it was found unchanged, immutable.

There is a strong tendency for Christians to imitate what is good in the world. We do not think that the acts of this world are all bad. However, while living in the world, Christians must make sure that their actions conform to the commandments of God. **What His word accepts, they must accept it. What His word rejects, they must reject it**. It is then that they will be the Christians God is proud of.

For example, the Lord asks not to take revenge, to leave Him the exclusivity of revenge. He asks Christians to be happy when one spread bad news about them because of Him. This warns Christians against any search for popular recognition. Those who wish to be praised in the world and those who are afraid of being looked down, cannot be the Christians that Jesus Christ seeks. The Lord asks the Christians to turn the second cheek after being slapped, to walk one more miles after being forced to make one, to give a second tunic after being deprived of the first. This is possible only if one possesses the Holy Spirit in oneself. And Christians must not find excuses and pretexts to avoid it. Likewise, the Lord will ask them to love their enemies and to greet them. They must obey to be His disciples. That is how they will strip themselves of the old human nature in favor of the new, divine, incorruptible one.

TO WALK IN THE SPIRIT

(Note: to walk in the Spirit = to live by faith)

«***Walk in the Spirit** and you shall not fulfill the lusts of the flesh*»
Galatians 5:16.

«*If we live in the Spirit, **let us also walk in the Spirit***»
Galatians 5:25.

Introduction

According to **Galatians 5:25** above, to walk in the Spirit comes from being born of the Spirit. We walk in the Spirit because we are born of the Spirit. Just as the pagan walks by the flesh because he is born of the flesh, the Christian must walk in the Spirit – who dwells in his spirit – because he is born of the Spirit.

The phrase "*walk in the Spirit*" is widely used in Paul's epistles and in evangelical and Pentecostal churches. And we must recognize from experience that there is a lot of confusion around this expression. First, because we do not see the Spirit as we would see a touchable object. So how do we walk according to someone we do not see? We are used to walking in the flesh because the man is made of flesh and bone clearly visible. Very honestly, at the beginning of Christian life, this phrase seems blurred in the young convert's head. Even if he mimics this expression, the reality is often too confused to the extent that few people have a life of irreproachable sanctification to serve as a guide. We must also recognize that of all the writers of the Scriptures, Apostle Paul is the only one to have spoken widely and deeply on *walking in the Spirit*. It can be understood because he was a lawyer in Israel. He had a very strong intellectual side, which explains in part that he signed and co-signed more than half of the New Testament books.

By *walking in the Spirit*, many often refer to hearing the voice of God, which is neither false nor exaggerated. But here too, there is so much confusion among Christians that this question is rarely mentioned in the sermons.

It is God who makes His voice heard by means of His Spirit who dwells in a Christian

The voice of God is not a disc that plays as soon as we click on the start button. God is a living being, sentimental, intelligent and active like any normal human, although visible contrary to God. Indeed according to the first commandment of Moses, God refuses to be represented by any form of image or sculpture whatsoever.

Many wonder how they could hear the voice of God. It is a healthy concern that must not worry the Christian beyond measure because it is the Lord who, above all, desires His sheep to hear His voice. He says:

> «*My sheep **hear My voice**, and I know them, and **they follow Me**. And I give to them eternal life, and they shall never ever perish, and **not anyone shall pluck them out of My hand**»* **(John 10:27-28).**

These words should reassure the Christian that the Lord will arrange for him, the Christian, to hear His voice and not that of the stranger. The Lord did not specify how He will proceed. And even in the Scriptures, no one has described or demonstrated the process by which the Lord made His voice heard. What is important to remember is that God speaks to His children and His children hear Him. Scripture and many experiences indicate that the Lord speaks in many ways. We will quote randomly: Scriptures (Bible), prophets, Christians, various ministers and messiahs, dreams, revelations, observations and noises, deductions, successes and failures, diseases, life and death, His creation overall. The list is not exhaustive. We also know that the Lord communicates with every Christian through a private window according to the individual call received. So the Lord will speak in such a different way to a prophet, an apostle, an evangelist, a teacher, a healer, a sentry, a people leader, a business leader, and so on. This is so that the Christian can recognize the voice of His Master in the midst of a multitude of voices. A child cannot ignore his mother's voice. He knows how to recognize it among a thousand. Similarly, a mother cannot ignore the call of her child. Yet the communion between the Lord and the Christians is deeper than between the mother and child. For even though the mother and child are close, they can't live one in the other as the Lord lives in the Christian by the Holy Spirit.

When it comes to listening to God, it is God who takes the initiative – not man – to make His voice heard, because the voice of God is not a recorded disk. **Just as no one can make a third party speak without the consent of the latter, one cannot make God speak without His consent**. To hear God, it is already necessary that God agrees to cooperate and that the Christian is in good mood and sanctification. The only word that a Christian, walking sideways, can hear from God is the disapproving silence followed, sometimes, by a disciplinary measure when he persists in misguidance. For example, the Scriptures testify that the Lord no longer spoke to King Saul after he disobeyed God (**1 Samuel 13:13-14**).

The voice of God has never contradicted Scripture. Frequent Scripture reading plus practical experience are strong references for evaluating any word that is supposed to come from God. Indeed, many words are attributed to God while they come from men and their traditions. Jesus in His time had already denounced this tendency among the scribes and Pharisees (**Matthew 15:6**). In the same way, many traditions, with appearances of virtue, have been introduced in Christian churches. The problem is that we seem to stick to these traditions more than to the word of God. It is indeed easy to obtain popular support in the church when one imputes to God the good practices of human traditions. But the Christian's focus on human traditions will lead him to confusion, because he will take what comes from men as coming from God. In addition to the example quoted by Jesus in **Matthew 15:6**, concerning the human traditions introduced by the Pharisees, one can quote "*Help yourself and the heaven will help you*" as one of the pagan traditions tolerated in the church. This thought is positive, with a great appearance of virtue, but it does not come from God and is nowhere reported in Scripture, even implicitly. In the time of Apostle Paul, the Jewish Christians from Asia were attempting to impose circumcision on the converted Gentiles, which Paul was strongly opposed to, arguing that Judaism could not be imposed on non-Jews. This is one of the grievances for which he was persecuted to the chains. Yet there is nothing wrong with circumcision. But although safe, its introduction was of human (Jewish) traditions and not of the will of God. It was a clever way to enslave Christians (**Galatians 2:4**). For once circumcision is accepted, another element would follow, then another, and so on until the whole assembly is under the control of individuals with selfish intentions.

God knows what part of the Scriptures the Christian understands and the part he does not understand. God will make sure that the Christian puts into practice the part of the Scriptures that he understands. He will have compassion when the Christian will falter on the unknown part of Scripture. In case of temptation or call not coming from Him, God allows the Christian to trust the Scriptures (the part he understands) to protect himself. If an appeal invites to steal, betray, false witness or other perversions such as adultery or murder, all that is condemned by Scripture, then the Christian will have to reject this call regardless of its consequences. God will be grateful to him for suffering in His name.

Apart from the word of God, two other ways enable the Christian to check the will of God. These are the circumstances and the inner feeling – peace or conscience's opposition. But neither of these means can oppose Scripture. When Scripture has already spoken clearly, it is always better to follow it. As far as the circumstances are concerned, it is clear that we cannot intervene in a situation that is hundreds of kilometers away, such as extinguishing a fire or assisting a person in need. In such cases, a prayer to God will suffice for the distant circumstances to arrange. No one can, in the name of God, ask for a hundred dollars when the person solicited does not have this money. These are circumstances that do not confirm the will of God. Similarly the urgency cannot push to steal or abuse under the pretext of a legitimate cause. God is powerful to arrange circumstances in favor of the Christian whatever the situation. As for the inner feeling favorable or not to a word imputed to God, we must make sure that our conscience is not disturbed. First, because consciousness is shaped by reading and practicing the word of God. On the other hand, according to a thorough analysis of the scriptures by a renowned Christian – Watchman Nee – consciousness is a faculty of the human spirit. As the Holy Spirit occupies the spirit of the Christian, we understand that the Holy Spirit will issue a warning signal when God's will is misjudged. Remember Daniel's amazement at the dream of the king of Babylon (**Daniel 4:16**). It was his conscience that was in turmoil. Let us also remember David's stupefaction when an emissary came to tell him the circumstances of King Saul's death (**2 Samuel 1:10-11**). It was still a reaction of consciousness. When consciousness awakens no signal, it is because there is no danger in what is presented to us. But when consciousness releases a negative signal, then caution is required. Very often, in such a case, the Lord puts in our intelligence a verse of Scripture or a word of wisdom corresponding to the situation. In the case where no verse comes to rescue, and the negative inner feeling persists, then we must grope, ready to stop in case of a strong alert. That is, reduce the margin of error as much as possible so that losses are minimal. Because every time we walk outside the will of God, we suffer a loss. However, one must not believe that a failure definitely remains a failure because, by means of failures, God teaches His children.

Attention, the inner feeling has nothing to do with sensations, impulses and excitations of the human body, as will be seen below.

To walk in the Spirit has nothing to do with the impulses, excitations and other sensations of the human body

It must be said again very strongly. Many Christians have been seduced by stories of sensations, excitement and impulses in the body. Attributing these feelings to the Lord is a big source of error. The Spirit of the Lord is not lodged in the senses and organs of man. The Spirit of the Lord is only lodged in the spirit of man as widely explained above. We know that the connection between the spirit of man and the members of the human body is not known even if we locate this spirit around the biological heart.

The devil is able to simulate sensations in the human body to seduce the Christian. The human body is not inaccessible to him. Satan is customary of attacks causing diseases. The Lord Jesus was often content to cast out a demon and the disease disappeared.

Apostle Paul says that he had to suffer a disability in his flesh because of an angel of Satan (**2 Corinthians 12:17**). We remember how the devil struck Job with ulcer. The physical body of man is a field that the devil often invests. To impute to God a physical excitement of the body is to open window to many excesses. Personally, I met Christians who went this way. The least I can say is that some were so confused that they needed the help of a psychiatrist.

We walk **in the Spirit using mainly the sword of the Spirit who is the Word of God**. When a message imputed to the Lord invites to transgress the Scripture, it is a trap of the devil. We must go away from it.

The sword of the Spirit – the Word of God – is the main weapon of the Christian against the traps of the enemy. Some will say: Why does the Lord let it go? The answer is provided by Scripture:

> «*If a prophet rises among you, or a dreamer of dreams, and gives you a sign or a wonder, and the sign or the wonder which he foretold to you occurs, saying, let us go after other gods which you have not known, and let us serve them, you shall not listen to the words of that prophet or that dreamer of dreams. **For Jehovah your God is testing you to know whether you love Jehovah your God with all your heart and with all your soul***» (**Deuteronomy 13:1-3**).

This passage from the Scriptures is very instructive because here the signs and miracles performed by the false prophet are fulfilled; whereas we are accustomed to doubt a prophet when the event announced by him does not happen. So the problem, in this case, is not in the result, but in the process: although the result is reached, the prophet sinned by calling to rally to gods other than Jehovah. In this case, the prophet and the result must be ignored by the Christian. This means that Scripture takes precedence over all circumstances. It is clear that in the example of the false prophet above, the devil arranged the circumstances to seduce the Christians. But by reading the Scriptures, the Christian will escape the devil's trick. In other words, the Lord does not intervene often because He is waiting for the Christian to protect himself by proclaiming Scripture. This is what Jesus did when He was tempted by the devil after forty days fast: at every mention of the Scriptures by the devil, Jesus replied by saying "*On the other hand, it is written ...*" and the devil capitulated because Jesus knew that *the devil only comes to steal and kill*. On this basis, Jesus rejected all the devil's talks despite an exact narration of the Scriptures by him.

If a Christian receives a sensation or an excitement from the body as a result of his prayer and discovers that the word of God is broken, he should not abide by it. It is very clear: God tests Him to know if **He loves Him with all His heart and soul**. We will see if this Christian loves his feelings rather than God.

Note: The sensations, impulses, heartbeats and other excitations of the human body have often accompanied Christians in their lives. But it must be pointed out that these excitations have never been the driving force for Christians to act in one way or another, but rather, the consequence of something. Let's remember the first sin in Eden Garden. It was after eating of the tree of knowledge of good and evil that Adam and Eve realized that they were naked. The feeling of nudity was the result of disobedience, not the process leading to disobedience. When David was close to take King Saul's life, he had a heartbeat of reprobation – inner feeling. It was not the heartbeat that incited him against the monarch. But the heartbeat made him understand that the act he was about to accomplish was compromising him. It's like the adrenaline that comes from a drama. Adrenaline is not the cause, but the awareness of the danger. Therefore, to impute to God an intention based on the sensation of the body is a source of confusion that the enemy can exploit for his benefit. We should avoid offering him such benefit.

To walk in the Spirit is to walk by the sword of the Spirit who is the Word of God

> «*Take the helmet of salvation, and **the sword of the Spirit, which is the word of God**» (**Ephesians 6:17**).

To begin with, let's say a word about what the Lord does not like: Introduce unilaterally in His church, human traditions supposedly virtuous. It is true that in many millennia of presence on earth, man has developed techniques, methods and processes to make his stay pleasant. But many of these traditions are not acceptable to God. What the Lord recommends to Christians is not to rely on methods just because men have always applied them successfully. The Lord expects Christians to only apply His laws. They are summarized in the Law of Moses and his amendments. Jesus made amendments to the Law of Moses concerning, among others, law of retaliation, the repudiation of the woman and the commandment *to love one another*. On all questions concerning his experience on earth, the Christian must apply the laws of God and only these.

According to **Ephesians 6:17**, *to walk in the Spirit* is to obey the commandments of the Lord because the word of God is *the sword of the Spirit*. Even if the world we live in has managed to solve some problem, God requires His children to adopt His only solutions according to His holy commandments. Thus the Christian will pass from death to life, from human nature to the divine nature (see full explanation above).

The more general passage from **Ephesians 4:25 to 6:18** states that *to walk in the Spirit is to*:

- Reject the lie and tell the truth to your neighbor
- Avoid sinning when angered
- Not give room to the devil
- Not steal, but work to help others
- Avoid uttering unhealthy words
- Not sadden the Holy Spirit
- Avoid bitterness, animosity, anger, clamor, slander, and all malice
- Show kindness and compassion
- Be imitators of God
- Walk in love
- Avoid any form of misconduct, any form of impurity or greed
- Avoid rudeness, insane words, buffoonery, but to rather offer thanksgiving
- Not be seduced by empty speeches

- Not share with the sons of rebellion (debauchees, impure, greedy, idolaters)
- Examine what is pleasing to the Lord
- Have nothing in common with the barren works of darkness, but to denounce them
- Watch over his conduct, not as fools, but as wise
- Redeem the time because the days are bad
- Not be without intelligence, but understanding what the Lord's will is
- Not get drunk with wine, but be filled with the Spirit
- Converse through psalms, hymns and spiritual songs; sing and celebrate the Lord with all his heart
- Always give thanks for everything to God the Father, in the name of the Lord Jesus Christ
- Submit to each other in the fear of Christ
- Submit to her husband, as to the Lord because the husband is the head of the woman, as Christ is the head of the Church, who is His body and of which he is the Savior
- Love his wife, as Christ loved the Church
- Obey his parents according to the Lord, for this is right. Honoring your father and mother to be happy and live long on the earth
- Not irritate his children, but to raise them by correcting and warning them according to the Lord
- Obey his boss in the world with fear and trembling, in the simplicity of heart, as in Christ. To serve them willingly as if we were serving the Lord and not men
- Act with fear and trembling with servants (employees); to abstain from threats, knowing that their Master and yours are in heaven and that before Him there is no consideration of persons

- Have at his loins the truth for a belt; wear the breastplate of justice; put as shoes at his feet the good dispositions which the gospel of peace gives; take in all circumstances the shield of faith with which to extinguish all the fiery darts of the Evil one; take also the helmet of salvation and the sword of the Spirit which is the Word of God
- Pray at all times in the Spirit with all kinds of prayers and supplications.

To walk in the Spirit has nothing to do with theories about when, where, why and how. It would be as to swallow indigestible doctrines. God wants simplicity and obedience in practice, because too much doctrine distorts reality and produces visionaries of nothingness. To walk in the Spirit is to simply obey God as every child must obey his father without saddening him. To walk in the Spirit is therefore not to grieve the Holy Spirit who is in us – for example by violating the prescriptions listed above. In case of external interference, the devil for example, the Lord will give the Christian the means to get out of it, to distinguish the true from the false, what is from Him and what is not (**1 Corinthians 10:13**). If the Christian cannot distinguish between what is of the Lord and what is of other source, his vision will be falsified; one could even doubt the presence of the Holy Spirit within this Christian. Only the Light of God, the Holy Spirit, can distinguish what comes from God and what comes from the devil. Christians should not be ashamed to ask the question of the effective presence of the unseen Holy Spirit within them, nor to fear God's answer to this question. It is better to start on the right foot, when the weather is good – before our death or the return of the Lord – rather than fleeing forward and discover, years later, that we have always said, "*Lord, Lord ...* "without really knowing Him.

Apostle Paul, the great exegete of the Scripture, knew how to organize his epistles in order to avoid false interpretation because, let's face it, he was mostly misunderstood by his contemporaries, to the point where Apostle Peter came to his aid (**2 Peter 3:15**). Apostle Paul structured his letters in the same way: (i) greeting (ii) introduction (iii) explanation (iv) conclusion and goodbye.

It is interesting to note that Paul's conclusions always addressed practical aspects so that the saints would not give in to daydreams and fantasies. Let us try to examine these practical aspects from Corinthians to Hebrews.

To walk in the Spirit according to 1 Corinthians 16:13-14
- Watch, remain steadfast in the faith, be men, strengthen oneself
- That among you, everything is done with love.

To walk in the Spirit according to 2 Corinthians 13:11
- Be in joy, strive for perfection, console oneself, have the same thought, live in peace.

To walk in the Spirit according to Galatians 6:1-10

- Gently restore the guilty brother
- Carry each other's burdens
- Let him who is taught in the Scripture share with the one teaching in all good things.
- Do not make fun of God
- Do not get tired of doing good
- Practice good to all, especially to the brothers in the faith.

To walk in the Spirit according to Ephesians 6:1-18

See above.

To walk in the Spirit according to Colossians 4:1-6

- Grant the servants what is right and just, knowing that you, too, have a Master in the sky
- Persevere in prayer, watch with thanksgiving
- Pray also for ministers and collaborators
- Behave wisely towards those outside. Redeeming time
- May your word be always accompanied by grace, seasoned with salt, to know how to respond to each one.

To walk in the Spirit according to 1 Thessalonians 5:8-22

- Be sober: put on the breastplate of faith and love, as well as the helmet of the hope of salvation
- Exhort one another and build one another
- Have consideration for those who work among us, who lead us in the Lord and who warn us. To have the highest esteem for them with love, because of their work. To be at peace between us

- Warn those who live in disorder, comfort those who are slaughtered, support the weak, use patience towards all
- Let no one render evil for evil; but always seek the good, either between us, or towards all
- Always be happy
- Pray continuously
- In all circumstances, give thanks
- Do not extinguish the Spirit
- Do not despise prophecies; but examine all things, remember what is good
- Refrain from evil in all its forms.

To walk in the Spirit according to 2 Thessalonians 3:1-15

- Pray for the rulers, that the word of the Lord may spread and be glorified, and that they may be delivered from foolish and wicked men; because not everyone has faith
- Get away from any brother who lives in disorder and not according to the tradition you have received from leaders (...) because if someone does not want to work, he should not eat either
- Do not get tired of doing good
- If someone does not obey what we say in this letter, take note of him and don't have a relationship with him, so that he is ashamed
- Do not think of him as an enemy, but warn him like a brother.

To walk in the Spirit according to 1 Timothy 6:1-20

- That the servants value their own masters worthy of all honor, so that the name of God and the doctrine are not slandered
- That those who have believers for masters do not despise them, under the pretext that they are brothers
- So if we have food and clothing, that will be enough for us
- Those who want to get rich fall into temptation, into the trap and into a host of senseless and pernicious desires, which plunge men into ruin and perdition

- Seek justice, piety, faith, love, patience, gentleness
- Fight the good fight of faith, seize eternal life
- Keep the command unblemished, without reproach, until the appearance of our Lord Jesus Christ
- Recommend to the rich of the present century not to be proud and not to put their hope in uncertain riches, but to put it in God who gives us all in abundance, for us to enjoy
- Do good, be rich in good works, have liberality, generosity, and so build up a beautiful and solid treasure for the future, in order to grasp the true life
- Keep the deposit, avoiding empty and profane speeches, and arguments of false science.

To walk in the Spirit according to 2 Timothy 4:2-5

- Preach the word, insist on any occasion, favorable or not, convince, resume, exhort, with all patience and instructing
- Be sober in everything, bear the sufferings, do the work of an evangelist, fulfill the Lord's service well.

To walk in the Spirit according to Titus 3:1-11

- Be submitted to governments and authorities, obey them, and be ready for any good work
- Do not be afraid of anyone, be peaceful, conciliatory, gentle towards all men
- Avoid crazy discussions, genealogies, discord, disputes about the law, because they are useless and vain
- Depart, after a first and second warning, from the one who causes divisions, for such a man is perverted, sins and condemns himself.

To walk in the Spirit according to Hebrews 13:1-18

- Persevere in fraternal love
- Do not forget the hospitality; because in exercising it, some, without knowing it, have housed angels

- Remembering prisoners, as if we were in prison with them, and those who are mistreated as being, too, in a body
- That marriage is honored by all, and the marriage bed free from defilement. For God will judge the debauched and adulterers
- That your conduct is not inspired by the love of money; to be content with his present goods, for God Himself said, I will not forsake nor abandon you
- Remember the leaders who told you the word of God; consider the outcome of their lives and imitate their faith
- Do not be lured by all kinds of foreign doctrines. For it is good for the heart to be established by grace, and not by foods that have been of no use to those who have used it.
- Through Christ, offer unceasingly to God a sacrifice of praise, that is to say the fruit of lips that confess His name
- Do not forget the beneficence and the liberality, because it is to such sacrifices that God takes pleasure
- Obey and be submissive to his leader. For they watch over the good of our souls, which they will have to give an account of. To make sure that they can do it with joy and not by murmuring, which would not be to our advantage
- Pray for leaders; because they are convinced of having a good conscience, with the will to behave well in all respects.

Important notice: by going through the practical tips above, some would be tempted to say that *it is impossible to execute these instructions*, which, at first sight, seems particularly restrictive for the natural man. But let's relax because God does not keep an accounting record of Christians successes and failures. What would be humanly understandable is not the mode of operation of the God of grace. He expects Christians to adopt the tendencies of the Spirit because He has put His Spirit in them. Without the Spirit of Christ, not only does a person not belong to Him, but it is impossible for him to honor His commandments. If God worked with an accounting record of successes and failures, there is no doubt that the people of the Bible would not have been saved (**Luke 18:13-14**), nor that one robber of the two men crucified with Christ in Golgotha. David would not have been forgiven after his crime of adultery. Moses neither. *For by grace Christian are saved through faith, and that not of themselves, it is the gift of god.* Merit or salary rewards a job, and grace rewards the absence of a meritorious work. God knows that Christians will have weaknesses and sins. The strength of salvation in Christ rests on the fact that *where sin abounded, grace did much more abound.* The Lord is asking us to have a posture of contrition which has nothing to do with a balance sheet of successes and failures. It is characteristic of the Pharisees and religious men to keep such records to boast of them as the Pharisee who boasted of tithing all his revenues, and of fasting twice a week (**Luke 18:13-14**). Such is not the doing of the God of grace. Apostle Paul made the above recommendations because the Holy Spirit was at work and not the natural man. In seeking perfection, the Christian will be led by the Holy Spirit to carry out His commandments. Failures will be numerous, but by persevering in faith, he will reach perfection to the glory of God the Father.

In conclusion, **to walk in the Spirit is essentially to use the sword of the Spirit which is the Word of God**; they are simple acts that everyday life makes possible for everyone. One does not need to live a life of sanctification in caves, to flee a corrupt world. This would be to violate the word of Christ who, in His last prayer to God, affirmed, "*I do not pray for You **to take them out of the world**, but for You to keep them from the evil*" (**John 17:15**).

All Christians are exhorted to walk in the Spirit to overcome the carnal tendencies as invasive as the world around. This is how they will keep a broken and contrite heart in front of God Almighty.

TO PRAY IN THE SPIRIT

«***Praying always*** *with all prayer and supplication* ***in the Spirit****, and watching to this very thing with all perseverance and supplication for all saints*»
Ephesians 6:18.

«*But you, beloved, building yourselves up in your most holy faith,* ***praying in the Holy Spirit***»
Jude 1:20.

As we have seen in the chapter *To walk in the Spirit*, to pray in the Spirit is also misinterpreted by many whereas it should not. Just look at the Scriptures to find out.

Many believe that *to pray in the Spirit* is to pray in tongues because tongues are a gift of the Holy Spirit. In all honesty, speaking in tongues can be considered as to pray in the Spirit. But if we stick to this configuration, we will miss the essential elements – note however that for Apostle Paul, the one who speaks in tongues prays with his (human) spirit and not in the Spirit (**1 Corinthians 14:14**).

Just as **to walk in the Spirit** is **to walk by the sword of the Spirit** who is the Word of God, **to pray in the Spirit** is also **to pray by the sword of the Spirit**. Clearly, it is about supplicating God according to His will expressed in the Scripture. The Scripture says:

«*This is the confidence that we have toward Him, that if we ask anything **according to His will**, He hears us. And if we know that He hears us, whatever we ask, we know that we have the petitions that we desired of Him*» (**1 John 5:14-15**).

Other translation:

> «*And this is the confidence that we have towards Him, that whatever we ask of Him, **agreeably to His will**, He heareth us. And if we are persuaded that He heareth us respecting what we ask of Him, we are confident of receiving presently the petitions which we asked of Him*» (**1 John 5:14-15/ Bible Murdoch**).

According to the above verse, God listens – agrees – to our prayer when we ask something **according to His will**, that is, a will perfectly expressed in the Bible. What divine will are we talking about? His commandments, no more no less. As we go through the Scriptures, we discover what God asks and orders to do. God is aware that the flesh cannot please Him. Rather than trusting our personal – carnal – abilities to honor God's commandments, let us ask God to help us satisfy them, and He will do so because *what is impossible for men is possible for God*. And "*It is God who works in you both to will and to do of His good pleasure*" (**Philippians 2:13**).

To be more convinced of this, let us go back to the sources of the Word to notice that it is in the same paragraph of the Scriptures that Paul said both to take the sword of the Spirit which is the Word of God, and to pray all time in the Spirit:

> «*And take the helmet of salvation, and **the sword of the Spirit, which is the word of God, praying always** with all prayer and supplication*

> ***in the Spirit***, *and watching to this very thing with all perseverance and supplication for all saints»* (**Ephesians 6:17-18**).

In exhorting *to pray in the Spirit with all perseverance and supplication*, Paul goes far beyond the speaking in tongues. Prayers in tongues are, for example, ineffective in group because no one will say amen to an incomprehensible prayer. The group prayers are done with intelligence and not in tongues as it is written: "*Yet in a church I desire to speak five words with my mind, so that I might also teach others, than ten thousand words in a tongue"* (**1 Corinthians 14:19**).

To pray in the Spirit is therefore to address to God all kinds of intelligent supplications with regard to the Bible. Let's ask what the Scriptures promise and God will listen to us. Any other prayer is selfish and passionate. And we know that the passionate prayers are rejected by God as it is written, "*You ask **and receive not, because you ask amiss, that you may spend it upon your lusts***" (**James 4:3**).

TO FREE IN THE SPIRIT

I do not know anyone on earth who can live and act freely as Jesus did during his earthly journey. He broke the storm, walked on the water, turned the water into wine, raised the dead, delivered the possessed, multiplied the bread, resisted King Herod and the lax and corrupt Jewish clergy. Nothing resisted Him in fact. He was free, really free. He said:

> «*If the Son shall make you free, you shall be free indeed*» (**John 8:36**).

Freed from the prejudices of the world

Skin, nationality, gender, culture, birth place, diploma, job and housing are cause of many prejudices. How many times have you suffered from being of low birth, low nationality, low facies? Yet you were aware of being up to the challenge. But unfortunately, something out of your control appeared and you were demoted. The Christian must reassure himself: Jesus Christ triumphed over the world and all its prejudices. He says indeed:

> «*In the world you (Christians) shall have tribulation, but be of good cheer. **I have overcome the world***» (**John 16:33**).

Which diploma owned Joseph, the Hebrew, promoted number two of ancient Egypt, then as dominant as the United States today? Yet Egypt did not lack eminent academicians who could ensure the mission of Joseph. Have they not invented the famous pyramids that have survived to this day, with their mummies, three thousand five hundred years after their construction? Joseph had no formal education since he had been a slave and a prisoner. The Hebrews of the time were considered a caste of untouchables since the Egyptians hated eating with them (**Genesis 43:32**). The story says however that Joseph did not only save Egypt from a great disaster, but also a seventy-people-family, the seed of Israel nation today.

What diploma owned Daniel, one of the Jewish deportees in Babylon? He had no formal diploma in a foreign city that would not have recognized his resume in any case. Yet by his genius, Daniel became the third VIP (very important personality) of the most powerful state of the world at the time, under several successive monarchs.

Many other cases can be recalled such as David slaying the giant Goliath while still a teenager (without warrior skills, he killed Goliath with the slingshot and the stone); such as Rahab, a former prostitute in Jericho, who became the ancestor of King David and Jesus Christ. All these examples should reassure Christians of their status: They do not have to fear not having the same pedigree as those of the world. They are special. They have a diploma that the world does not have: the Holy Spirit.

Freed from the tyranny of good manners and fashion effects

We must recognize that good manners are also sources of prejudices and discriminations in this world. Thus the populations of the big cities consider those of the other cities as barbarians, wild, ignorant, rough and manner-less. Jesus Himself was accused of being from a gloomy city of Nazareth in Galilee, of eating with tax collectors, of not washing hands before meals. All these good manners are pretty to see. At a time when absolute monarchies dominated the world, each social class was distinguished by a dress code in addition to bodily gestures of courtesy. But for the Lord, these rituals and good manners are not primordial anymore. Christians are called to free themselves from their tyranny. Do you eat at times not indicated by human tradition? No problem. Do you want to celebrate God outside of the dedicated days of worship? Feel free. Do you want to eat meat when the vegetarian diet is de rigueur? Feel free. Have you been told that you need to apply a precautionary measure before you commit? Go for it! The Lord will be with you. *Where the Spirit of the Lord is, there is freedom*. Have you been told that such food is favorable or unfavorable in this context? Let be guided by the Spirit and not by good manners. You are first of all the crown princes of the kingdom of heaven. Apostle Paul had already rebelled against the tyranny of these traditions. He said for example:

> «*But now, knowing God, but rather are known by God, **how do you turn again to the weak and beggarly elements to which you again desire to slave anew? You observe days and months and times and years.** I fear for you, lest*

> *somehow I have labored among you in vain. Brothers, I beseech you, be as I am; for I am as you»* (**Galatians 4:9-12**).

Sometimes, good manners have the unacknowledged purpose of subjugating docile and fragile people. It is a shame to find these shameful doings in the Church of Jesus Christ. Apostle Paul rebelled against these methods in harsh terms as follows:

> **«*For you endure if anyone enslaves you, if anyone devours, if anyone takes from you, if anyone exalts himself, if anyone strikes you in the face*.** *I speak according to dishonor»* (**2 Corinthians 11:20-21**).

Christians are free because Jesus has set them truly free. Amen.

Freed from the tyranny of science

As citizens of the kingdom of heaven, Christians should not be surprised to experience situations rarely mentioned in the world. Good or bad inextricable situations will happen to them. The kingdom of heavens being different from the earth, Christians should not be surprised that the laws of science could often not prevail where they live. By multiplying bread, turning water into wine, walking on water, Jesus showed that the laws of science are pointless compared to the kingdom of heavens. That is, the laws of science could lose their effects on Christians.

In interrupting the storm, Jesus was also showing that He was more competent than all the weather stations on earth. The latter can at best predict a storm, but we have never heard that a weather station had interrupted a storm like Jesus did.

Christians must not lock themselves into human boundaries of knowledge. Let them stop suffering because the Lord is above science.

Freed from the tyranny of holy days, holy places and holy meals

The man is naturally inclined towards religion. Many believe that this tendency is to fill the void left in the spirit of our ancestors Adam and Eve after the Fall. It is however a reality that the human being tends to develop a religious activity. He is superstitious. This explains why, despite the call of Jesus and His disciples not to erect holy days, places and meals, Christians persist in doing so. Let's see what Jesus said in His time:

> «*The hour is coming when you shall neither worship the Father in this mountain nor yet at Jerusalem. (...) But the hour is coming, and now is, when **the true worshipers shall worship the Father in spirit and truth**, for the Father seeks such to worship Him. God is a spirit, and they who worship Him must worship in spirit and in truth*» (**John 4:21-24**).

According to the Law of Moses, every Jew had to pray the face turned towards the holy city of Jerusalem. Commemorations under the Law could only be done in Jerusalem. Therefore, these solemnities were occasions for regrouping Jews from diaspora in Jerusalem. In addition to the holy place of Jerusalem, the days of the said commemorations were also holy days.

But Jesus came to announce that the earthly Jerusalem was no longer a holy city in the eyes of God the Father, nor any other place on earth. Apostle Paul drives the point by comparing this earthly Jerusalem to the spiritual figure of Hagar, the slave of Sarah (**Galatians 4:25**). For Jesus, the worshipers His Father seeks – the spiritual sons of Sarah – are the ones who worship the Father in spirit and in truth. Thus Jesus released his Christians from the tyranny of the holy places and days to which, alas for their misfortunes, the spiritual sons of Hagar – the inhabitants of the earthly Jerusalem – continue to submit.

Jesus has in fact released Christians from all tyrannies, including that of holy meals. When asked about it, Apostle Paul answered:

> « *I know, and am persuaded by the Lord Jesus, that **there is nothing unclean of itself**: but to him that esteemeth any thing to be unclean, to him it is unclean*» (**Romans 14:14/ Bible 1769Authorized Version**).

> «*Therefore **let no one judge you in food or in drink, or in respect of a feast, or of the new moon, or of the sabbaths**. For these are a shadow of things to come, but the body is of Christ* (**Colossians 2:16-17**).

> «*If then you died with Christ from the elements of the world, **why, as though living in the world, are you subject to its ordinances: Touch not, taste not, handle not**; which things are all for corruption in the using, according to the commands and doctrines of men? These things indeed have a reputation of wisdom in self-imposed worship and humility, and unsparing severity of the body, **but are not of any value for the satisfying of the flesh**»* (**Colossians 2:20-23**).

The Christian is thus released from the worship of holy days, holy places and holy meals.

Concretely, you can eat pork when people around consider it impure, while avoiding to provoke them – do it thus in private. You can eat beef in a world of vegetarians.

For the sake of the weak, however, he who esteems holy a day, a place or a meal, let him do it freely for God, without making others suffer, to avoid unnecessary conflicts.

The Lord knows that appearances are deceptive. What distinguishes a true Christian from a sorcerer disguised as a Christian? Nothing. Both can be confused. By getting rid of the tyranny of holy days, places and meals, the Lord is allowing us to live relaxed and free. He no longer wants caricatures of worshipers, mountain and caves worshipers. He wants worshipers in spirit and in truth for His Father.

Freed to learn everything

Have you not been barred from a professional career because you did not have the required diploma? Many have suffered this discrimination. A strong scientific base is usually required for technical vocational training such as accountancy, computer science, medicine, aeronautics, etc.

Far from us to say that human systems of selection are not good. On the contrary, they are. What we want to point out is that the Lord is advising His children not to become discouraged if they do not have the requested diploma for a training course. It's all about learning a job. There are indeed strict certification programs. But there are many other opportunities to be trained without going through the traditional certification program. This is self-learning. May Christians feel free to learn what is worthy of interest.

Believe me, there are many training courses that do not require a certificate. Christians will have many choices. But still, if the Lord puts in the heart of the Christian to attend a training course, whether or not he has the required ertificate, this Christian must thank the Lord and ask Him how to proceed. The Lord will show him the way. There are indeed many diploma equivalences. The Lord knows them all, even if the world ignores them or pretends to ignore them.

The Christian is free to take advantage of all the opportunities offered for training, whatever the field. Music is a field where many Christians exercise their talents without necessarily having the required diploma. Perhaps because in music matters, inspiration is more solicited than anything else; and inspiration is not dependent on the diploma. However if in music, one can progress without diploma, many other sectors can allow it. It will probably take more effort for the self-taught – it is not a certainty – but in the end, he will succeed.

That Christians feel free to learn everything according to their desire and availability. With the Lord Jesus Christ, everything is possible.

DO NOT GRIEVE THE HOLY SPIRIT, ESPECIALLY NOT!

«***Do not grieve the Holy Spirit of God***, *by Whom you are sealed until the day of redemption*»
Ephesians 4:30.

«*But he who blasphemes against the Holy Spirit never shall have forgiveness,* **but is liable to eternal condemnation**»
Mark 3:29.

The Holy Spirit has a discreet ministry because He is invisible, unlike the angel who made himself visible to the patriarchs, unlike Jesus Christ who announced the gospel in a body similar to ours. God has been represented by the angel (visible); Jesus Christ came to reveal the gospel of God in a visible human body. But the Holy Spirit is an invisible Actor. And the invisible actor works in discretion. The action of the Holy Spirit is therefore discreet and less noisy. No one can portray the Holy Spirit because He is invisible.

In passing the relay to the Holy Spirit, in the pursuit of His post-crucifixion work, Jesus Christ warns Christians not to begrudge an actor as discreet as the Holy Spirit. Jesus, because He was visible, could be invaded and contested. Each time He answered and clarified. This was the case, for example, when Peter was deeply worried about who could be saved if it was impossible for men. This was again the case when Peter loudly declared that he was ready to die to protect Jesus Christ against the Pharisees.

No one can contest the Holy Spirit who is invisible. This reality requires Christians to be discreet and serious in their sanctification because they are dealing with a discreet Actor. Here is the essential point: When a person is angry, we can see on his face or his gestures how much he has been affected, and act accordingly. But if we anger the Holy Spirit, we have no indication of the fault committed. It is after a considerable delay that it can be deduced that the Holy Spirit had been saddened. This was the case of King Saul of Israel whose contact with God was interrupted after he disappointed Him. On the other hand, God spoke continually to David, Saul's successor. God even allowed David, still unknown, to play the harp to deliver King Saul from his torments.

The Holy Spirit dwelling in the spirit of man (spiritual heart), making Him sad is to go against his own heart. Jesus said, "*Where your treasure dwells, **there will be your heart**,*" a way of giving man's heart a very great importance. Jesus again said, "*For out of the heart come evil thoughts, murders, adulteries, fornications, thefts, false witness, blasphemies*" (**Matthew 15:19**). The heart is an organ dear to God. He who keeps his heart in perfect condition, keeps his soul under control. To sadden the Holy Spirit, who resides around the heart, is to deprive oneself of an important support for the heart. He is not only a Comforter, but also a Physician because the Holy Spirit has received from the Lord the mission to deliver us from the terrible disease of ignorance. To imagine an abandoned heart is to open window to all kinds of perversions according to **Matthew 15:19**, and incurring severe judgments in the present century and at the end of time.

PRACTICE WITH THE HOLY SPIRIT

The Christian is always focused on things from above

> «*If then you were raised with Christ, **seek those things which are above**, where Christ is sitting at the right hand of God. **Be mindful of things above**, not on things on the earth*» **Colossians 3:1-2**.

> «*But if you have bitter jealousy and strife in your hearts, do not glory and lie against the truth. **This is not the wisdom coming down from above, but is earthly, sensual, devilish**. (...) But the wisdom that is from above is first truly pure, then peaceable, gentle, easy to be entreated, full of mercy and good fruits, without partiality and without hypocrisy*» **James 3:14-17**.

May Christians stop blaming themselves as if they were impostors. That they are not afraid to display their status in this world, a status recalled by Jesus Christ and as above His apostles from Paul to James. Jesus said that Christians were no longer of this world (**John 17:14-16**). By this declaration, Jesus set many things. Christians must question the scope of this statement. What does it really mean *to be no longer of this world*? It is very unfortunate that Christians do not think about the scriptures as they do for other issues of life. Many Christians have a driving license after a theoretical and practical exam. We know what it requires as a learning and memory effort to pass this exam. But many of these Christians are unable to memorize the essential verses of the Bible. The Lord's judgment of these Christians will be severe. Christians are content to pass on the holy Scriptures as if they were dealing with a storybook, or a monotonous music. This is sad and reprehensible.

Christians must live the Christian life as desired by the Lord and recalled by the apostles. From Paul to James, a common denominator appears: **things from above**. In other words, although living on earth, Christians must consecrate thoughts and interests to the things above, and make them a constant concern. Apostle Paul exclaims, "***Be mindful of things above**, not on things on the earth*" while James complains of this "***Wisdom not coming down from above, but that is earthly, sensual, devilish***".

The world will certainly take you for a mentally retarded. No matter, Christians must stay the course. Jesus says, " *Where your treasure dwells, there will be your heart* " By this phrase the Lord called His disciples to seek things from above, not to amass their treasures on earth, which are exposed to theft, to worms and rust (**Matthew 6:19-20**).

The Christian must assume the fact of living out of step with the world. The consequences of this life do not rest on him. Jesus Christ will assume and take everything on Him. The drama of many Christians is to anticipate the consequences of their actions in this world, caring about what the people around will think of them. Such should not be their problem. They must be content to live in accordance with the will of God. God will assume the consequences of their consecration.

The apostle Paul states:

> «*Therefore put to death your members which are on the earth: fornication, uncleanness, passion, evil desire, and covetousness which is idolatry. (...) Do not lie to one another, having put off the old man with his deeds and having put on the new, having been renewed in knowledge according to the image of Him who created him (new man)*» (**Colossians 3:5-10**).

The conclusion of the Apostle indicates that no Christian is exempt from this requirement of sanctification: *There is neither* **Greek nor Jew, circumcision and uncircumcision, foreigner, Scythian, slave or freeman**, *but Christ is all things in all* (**Colossians 3:11**).

Put everything down at the feet of the Lord

Many Christians find it difficult to put everything back into the hands of the Lord, especially when facing a thorny problem. The world has accustomed us to fight with different means including: school, experience and circumstances. It is not common to hear someone in trouble saying that he is going to pray. He takes the problem head to head as the saying goes: *You have to strike while the iron is hot.*

To put everything in the hands of the Lord is to pray and trust Him completely for the future. Do not forget, but stay alert. This is difficult for the pagans, but not for Christians, provided that they truly believe the Lord God will bring them out of a complicated and inextricable situation.

Christians who fight with the weapons of the flesh are always defeated. Those who put everything back to the Lord triumph. Those who fight with the weapons of the flesh – school and experience – will claim glory if successful. While those who give everything to the Lord, will give all the merit and glory to the Lord and only Him. This is why they triumph while carnal-oriented Christians fail.

The devil will attack and bring down Christians who are reluctant to lay everything down at the feet of the Lord. Suppose a Christian's live is a successful one: good salary, pretty house, wife and children doing well. In the mind of this Christian, it is the norm. Imagine then everything collapses around him: job loss, over-indebtedness, rents hard to honor. It is quite possible that the family unit will take a hit if misunderstanding increases at home. Should we try shortcuts to hold firm? Should we sell our soul to the devil as many pagans do? It is here the perseverance of the saints: to confide everything to the Lord and to accept all that will happen, the heart always joyful, without anxiety, to humiliate Satan, the accuser of the Christians and author of all their misfortunes. If the Lord wants a Christian to go a luxury-less life, he must accept without murmuring. It is his destiny desired by the Lord. He does not have to set a high standard to keep up with the times where the world thinks there are princes and others. The Lord can humble the Christian, just to teach him to live by faith in difficult conditions. May this Christian not imagine that he is being punished for serious misconduct. Job did not commit any fault, yet the devil treated him like a vomit. In the end, Job triumphed and the name of God was glorified to the shame of the devil.

The new heart according to God

*«Let not **your heart** be troubled, neither let it be afraid»* **John 14:27**.

«Rejoice evermore. (...) In everything give thanks, for this is the will of God in Christ Jesus concerning you» **1 Thessalonians 5:16 ; 18**.

By far I understood that by asking Christians to put everything at His feet, the Lord contributes to the health of these people. Let us remember the statement of Jesus: "*For out of the heart come evil thoughts, murders, adulteries, fornications, thefts, false witness, blasphemies*" (**Matthew 15:19**). The heart is a place of life that regulates the blood in the body. The heart plays a central role in maintaining a perfectly healthy body. When overloaded, the heart works badly. In all honesty, when the heart suffers, the whole human body suffers. All internal organs of the body then operate in slow motion.

On the other hand, a healthy heart makes the body light and supple. Many wrongly treated infections can weaken the heart in the long term. But there are other, much more formidable threats: the worries of life. For example, bad news on a regular basis, a succession of failures humans call 'bad luck'. In the elderly or sensitive souls, a succession of bad news affects the health of the heart with disastrous consequences on the whole body.

By exhorting Christians to put everything down at His feet, Jesus spares them the worries described above. Speaking of a Christian whose sanctification was excellent as far as I know him, his doctor said of him that his heart was like that of an athlete. One way to say that the pulse of this Christian has not changed over the years. But this Christian practiced no sport to my knowledge. He took pleasure in putting everything at the Lord's hands. His attitude irritated his contemporaries who criticized him for not being sufficiently worried when problems occured.

This is the problem of many Christians. They believe that solution is all about human effort. The Lord says that it is by faith that the Christian will find solutions to his problems, so he will live quietly.

Let's continue Paul's exhortation in **Colossians 3**:

> *«**3:12** Therefore, as the elect of God, holy and beloved, **put on tender feelings of mercy, kindness, humbleness of mind, meekness, long-suffering**.*

3:13 Forbearing one another and forgiving yourselves; if anyone has a complaint against any, as Christ forgave you, so also you do.

*3:14 And above all these things **put on love, which is the bond of perfectness**.*

*3:15 **And let the peace of God rule in your hearts, to which you also are called in one body**, and be thankful.*

*3:16 **Let the word of Christ dwell in you richly in all wisdom**, teaching and admonishing one another in psalms and hymns and spiritual songs, singing with grace in your hearts to the Lord»* (**Colossians 3:12-16**).

These words of exhortation are addressed to blameless Christians. Not that these Christians have no problem in their lives, but because these Christians are used to putting everything back in the hands of the Lord, in all situation they go through.

By saying, "*Let not your heart be troubled*" Jesus indicates that He wants Christians to live with a perfectly healthy heart. Thus, when the spiritual heart is in good health, the biological heart also does not take long to be in good health, as will be the whole human body.

The Christian is a bulwark against the destruction of the world by the devil

«*The earth also was corrupt before God, and the earth was filled with violence. And God looked upon the earth. And, behold, it was corrupted!* **For all flesh had corrupted its way upon the earth**. *And God said to Noah, the end of all flesh has come before Me,* **for the earth is filled with violence through them**. *And, behold, I will destroy them with the earth*» (**Genesis 6:11-13**).

«**The men of Sodom were wicked and sinners before Jehovah, exceedingly so**» (**Genesis 13:13**). «*Then Jehovah rained upon Sodom and upon Gomorrah* **brimstone and fire, from Jehovah out of the heavens**» (**Genesis 19:24**).

«*You Israelites shall not walk in the ways of the nation which I cast out before you.* **For they committed all these things, and therefore I loathed them**» (**Leviticus 20:23**).

Let us not be surprised that the world almost never remembers Jesus except at Christmas, Easter and other Christian holidays. Let us not be surprised that even Christians are astonished, in the evening, that a whole day has passed without a thought for the Lord Jesus Christ. How, indeed, can we forget the presence of the One who, through His Spirit in us, accompanies us every day to the end of time?

Do not look long for answers to these different questions. It is the prince of the power of the air, Satan, who blinds the intelligence of the humans. Satan's goal is to keep men and women away from Christ as much as possible. One of his mottos is *Everything but Christ*.

How can God be ignored on the earth He has created? Yet that's what the devil wants to perpetuate. The reason is that by keeping humans away from Christ, they will multiply acts contrary to the holiness of God, such as the divination by which we worship other gods beside God Almighty.

The devil keeps in memory some tragic events that have mourned humanity. These include the deluge that destroyed the entire human race except eight people: Noah, his wife, three sons and three stepdaughters. The Scripture also mentions Sodom and Gomorrah, that ancient city which was consumed by fire and from which only three people escaped: Lot and his two virgin daughters. These two tragedies occurred because humans multiplied abominable acts in the face of the Almighty God.

Also in history, the Scripture evokes the reason why the Canaanites were driven out of their territory for the benefit of the Israelites: they'd multiplied abominable acts before God. It was the same reason that led to the deportation of the sons of Israel to Assyria and Babylon amid terrible suffering: famine, plague, mutilations, disembowelings, killings, rapes, devastation, destruction, poverty, and so on.

The more men multiply the abominations on the earth, the more the anger of God ignites with terrible consequences. The devil knows it all too well. History gives him reason. Let us remember the plan of the corrupted prophet Balaam to draw the divine curse on the Israelites, and to stoop their campaign of conquering the promised land. The prophet incited the Moabites to compromise the Israelites in the debauchery and consumption of meat sacrificed to idols:

> *«You have there those who hold the teachings of Balaam, who taught Balak to cast a stumbling-block before the sons of Israel, to **eat things sacrificed to idols and to commit fornication**» (**Revelation 2:14**).*

Being the light of the world, the Christian becomes a bulwark against the extermination plans of the devil. The Christian must understand that his faith is a factor that Satan fears because it spoils his plans. Satan will not sit idly before the Christians. As a result, there is a lot of intimidation against Christians. One of the methods used by the devil is to make Christians look like backsliders, telling everyone that the Bible dates from a bygone era and that today is the age of the Internet, satellites and modernity.

The Christian must not be intimidated by those around him who take pleasure in calling him mad. There are many Christians who hid in their slums for fear of being treated as crazy. By asking Christians to carry their cross, Jesus Christ knew that these sad occasions would multiply. The Christian must stand firm despite the adversity, shame and humiliation of the world around him. Let him not give up, for that is what Satan is looking for above all. Perseverance will bring Christians to triumph over all forms of adversity.

Because of the presence of Lot, God put on gloves. He made sure that Lot, Abraham's nephew, was safe before burning Sodom and Gomorrah. It is a habit of the Almighty. He always puts His saints safe before attacking a rebellious city.

The presence of a Christian in a city, a company, an organization, helps to secure the place, which irritates Satan the destroyer.

Christians are therefore called to pursue a stainless sanctification in order to preserve a place, a company, etc. It is true that at the end of time, God will send His angels to remove the saints, at the sound of the trumpet, before destroying forever the present impious world.

But in the meantime, Christians are invited to sanctify themselves seriously and to persevere in this way.

Christians are wonderful creatures

> *«I (David) will praise you; **for I am fearfully and wonderfully made**; your works are marvelous and my soul knows it very well»* **Psalms 139:14**.

These remarks were made by David, king of Israel, at the time of the Levitical priesthood to which the Scripture gives a mere symbolic value. The Levitical priesthood was given to the sons of Israel while waiting for the advent of the perfect priesthood of Jesus Christ. We can therefore say that believers of the New Covenant are more valuable – because of their higher priesthood – than believers of the Old Covenant.

So if David received in Spirit that he was a wonderful creature, how much more will today's Christians be, if not more so.

The Christian having the Spirit of God in him, how could he not be a wonderful creature? Because John the Baptist was the prophet who prepared the Lord's arrival on earth, Jesus Christ describes him as the greatest human of the Old Covenant. Would we be embarrassed to learn that Christians are wonderful creatures because of the Holy Spirit dwelling in them? No way! We affirm according to Scripture that Christians are wonderful creatures.

From then, let us reveal other truths. As wonderful creatures, Christians should adhere to the Bible rules of sanctification from one chapter to another.

Let's be honest to say that God's command is not easy to obey. Not that it is impossible – because the difficulty is lessened by the Holy Spirit within the Christian – but it is the opinion of the world around us which is difficult to stand. Let's face it, many Christians are ashamed to testify publicly for fear of being mocked by the surrounding world.

As a wonderful creature, the Christian has an impressive arsenal to meet all the challenges that will arise. Did God not tell him to worry not because it is the heathen who are worried about the things of the earth? But in all things, the Christian is invited to give thanks, then to present all kinds of requests to God who will know how to bless him beyond imagination.

The Holy Spirit always makes you happy

«*Rejoice in the Lord always. Again I say, rejoice!*» **Philippians 4:4**.

«*Rejoice evermore*» **1 Thessalonians 5:16**.

When reading these words of Apostle Paul, the honest Christian is strongly tempted to wonder if the author really meant these words in this world where, as Paul himself acknowledged it, Christians live like sheep regularly delivered to the slaughterhouse (**2 Corinthians 4:8-11**). How can one be happy in this trouble world? Is the apostle's recommendation not surrealistic? In appearance, one would be forced to admit it, but in truth, as explained below, the apostle translated the feeling of God to His children whom He cherishes. Christians must always be happy.

Who do we believe we are to receive the Spirit of God in the earthen vessel of man? Who do we believe we are to be invited to sit on the throne of God (**Revelation 3:21**)? Is God ashamed to put man in such high esteem? It's a mystery. However the Scriptures are clear: despite the Christian be intimidated by the world around, God takes him in high esteem to the point of reserving a place for him on His glorious throne. And that's what counts. By placing His Holy Spirit in the Christian, God proves that He has esteem for him. It is a fact that goes beyond all evidences and demonstrations.

Imagine that in your neighborhood, people have got used to looking down on you, because they think that you are of very tiny importance. By this attitude, you end up convincing yourself that you are nothing. Imagine that afterwards, the governor, passing through your neighborhood, spends five minutes discussing with you at home. What do you think will be the attitude of people towards you from now? Although your situation has not changed, people will take a different look on you. They'll think it's for a good reason that the governor stopped at your place in the middle of so many witnesses. From that moment, they will stop looking down on you. This is said: to be reconciled with the truth. If in your own eyes you do not have high esteem of yourself, the governor's attitude is the evidence of the contrary, a true demonstration.

If God felt that the Christian is worth receiving His Spirit, the Christian no longer has to consider himself worthless. He is highly esteemed by God. More importantly, the Christian must congratulate himself and rejoice. As much as the man of the above anecdote will boast of having received the governor, even for a handful of minutes, so much the Christian must rejoice to receive the Spirit of God, not for a handful of minutes, but for eternity.

The Christian must constantly rejoice. The Christian can, however, invoke unfavorable circumstances to justify his apathy, if for example, he suffers insults in the midst of tribulations. But the Lord invites him to put everything in His hands and rejoice. If the Christian took to heart everything he suffered from the world, he would not be safe. His heart would weaken, dragging with him the rest of the body. Those with a fragile heart will soon see their overall health decline.

Speaking of the world, Jesus said, "*If they reject Me, they will reject you*". "*It's not you they reject, it's Me they reject.*" With these words, Jesus invites Christians not to take to heart all the frustrations they will experience as sons of God. Otherwise, their hearts would not keep fit.

By putting all the frustrations back into the hands of the Lord, the heart becomes lighter and regains all its strength and vigor. The Christian is not responsible for the consequences of his choosing to follow the Lord. It is up to the Lord Jesus Christ to deal with these consequences. The Christian does not have to assume before those of the world. Jesus Christ will speak for him. The Lord said, when it comes to the persecution of Christians: "*When they deliver you up, take no thought how or what you shall speak; **for it shall be given you in that same hour what you shall speak**. For it is not you who speak, but **the Spirit of your Father who speaks in you**"* (**Matthew 10:19-20**).

God wants the hearts of his children to be perfectly healthy. Christians do not have to face the consequences of their choice to follow Jesus and the resulting sanctification. Only sanctification must concern Christians. Consequences belong to Jesus Christ.

Quarrels must stop, no matter who they are – people of the world, colleague or boss, relationship, family, etc. If the Christian manages these hazards, his heart will not last long. Let him leave everything to Jesus and watch over the only burden that counts for God: sanctification without which no one will see the Lord. The heart of this Christian will always be in perfect health and his body will follow the trend. Many diseases will stop crushing him, and the temple of the Holy Spirit, he is, will be better off.

FACE-TO-FACE MEETING WITH THE HOLY SPIRIT

First face-to-face meeting

When you agree to host a man, what rule does he observe when living in your home? His or yours as the owner? The proprietor's rule of course, was my answer to this question of the Holy Spirit. *What will happen if the host persists in going against the rule set by the proprietor? Will he be kept on the premises? No,* was my answer. *He will be expelled.*

How is it that men and women do not observe the rules of life that I have established on the land I have created? These rules are in the Bible. Will I let them continually trample My Holy Word on My land? This is why there are many deaths before term, as well as other calamities that strike humans. Even Christians who violate My command on earth do not escape it. Such is My holiness and I do not accept the person of anyone.

Humans know how to react when someone does not respect the rules of his host. They expel the offender. However, they do not believe that I can oppose them the same severity when they continually violate My law before

My face, on the land that I have created. They even claim that the land comes from a Big-Bang. If humans control the Big-Bang so much, why do they not master the structure of the atom yet, nor prevent death from hitting them?

Apostle Paul has warned you perfectly against the violation of My commandments. For young people who do not honor their parents, it is a reduced life expectancy. For husbands who do not like their wives, there are blocked prayers. However, in spite of My punishments, they do not come back seriously from bad behavior.

How do you think you can sit at the same table as Abraham, you who cannot stand the trials I send to strengthen your faith? I did not promise anyone a painless life on earth. All My prophets have suffered. Myself I was not spared during My earthly journey. How does the Christian think he can sit at the same table as Abraham and the patriarchs, when he cannot bear any trial? How does he think to enter My kingdom with a gold spoon in his mouth? Will I take away this Christian on the trumpet of the angel?

I demand that My Christians practice a sanctification relentlessly and I will take them away on the sound of the trumpet. May they seek Me as the apple of their eyes, for I will not take him who does not wait for My coming, nor who is not eager to enter the heavenly Jerusalem for the wedding of the Lamb.

May those who are on the right foot persevere. I am faithful. Maranatha! I am coming soon with My retribution.

Second face-to-face meeting

When you pray to Me, do you think you deserve answer? Whoever prays, does he deserve My answer? Does the owner of a property pray to enjoy this property or simply dispose of it as he pleases?

Many of My servants speak to Me, sometimes with exasperation, as if they were at the end of themselves. Do they think they have rights? Do they have the right to be heard or rather do they hope for My grace? Have you read in My Word that prayer gives rights or graces? Some even threaten to leave the priesthood if I do not answer their prayers. Will I give in to this blackmail?

When a condemned person asks for grace, does he exercise his right to life or does he hope for the grace of authority? Will authority not react as he pleases? Will the authority succumb to a threat or some form of blackmail? I am surprised that My Christians come to Me with some kind of urgency as if I have to answer them. Terrestrial authorities take time to respond to your graceful requests. Shall I deprive myself?

Read My Word. Did I not expel Adam from the Garden of Eden after condemning him to return to the dust from which he was created? Have I not deprived man of the most basic rights of life? I told the man that it is with the sweat of his brow that he will eat his bread; and to the woman that it is in the pain that she will give birth. Are not eating and giving birth essential to life on earth? Did the advent of Jesus Christ exonerate the Christian from these hardships? Do you know a Christian who eats without perspiring or a Christian woman who gives birth without suffering?

On leaving this earth, I asked My Christians to address supplications to the Father in My name. But how can they turn graceful prayer into a command?

When you address a gracious request to the authority, does he not act in all discretion as he sees fit? Why are My Christians speaking to My Father so casually as if they had a right to claim?

The prayer will never change into an order. Prayer remains a graceful request. When I answer the prayer of a Christian, I do not give him a right, but a mercy. If, while waiting for My answer, He does not respect Me, live for example in sin, will I be attentive to his prayer? When you pray, expect a positive answer from My Father, take an attitude of contrition because it is not about rights, but grace.

Just as the authority to whom you have sent a graceful request, will resist you if he realizes that you are multiplying reprehensible acts, My Father will also resist the Christian who does not sanctify himself according to His holiness, all these things are perfectly explained in the Scriptures.

When you pray, wait for My answer in the breaking and contrition knowing that you hope for graces and not rights. Because rights are deserved while grace is not.

Third face-to-face meeting

I am God and My sheepfold is perfectly fenced. No one will go through the window like a thief. I asked those who love Me to go through the narrow door. But many act as if there is an alternative to this door. Many have in mind the large commercial areas accessed by several doors: north, south, east and west. There are no more access doors to My Sheepfold. There is only one and I stand there, my eyes wide open. I monitor the entrance like you monitor access to your earthly houses.

Can you enter a man's house without being invited? If so, then you are a thief. If you know how to protect your earthly houses with locks, do you think that I, Jesus, will not know how to do it on My sheepfold? Is it not disrespectful to Me?

That nobody imagines being able to reach My sheepfold through a back door. No one will enter without My consent. The money and the bulldozer can do nothing. I am alive. May the Christian accept the conditions of access to My Sheepfold. They are not difficult because My burden is light and My yoke is easy.

Whoever perseveres to the end will be saved.

Fourth face-to-face meeting

You do not examine My Word to explore its content. You know how to explore contracts between humans. But nothing like it for My Word while it is alive, even more alive than the sky and the earth that will pass like a garment. You should have pondered the different implications of the statement that "I am the Lion of the tribe of Judah". But you do not do anything! What is a lion? Should have been an essential question of curiosity, but on the contrary, it became a pseudonym in the minds of many Christians. I repeat, I am neither a junk lion nor a paper lion. I am a real Lion. Satan walks about like a roaring lion, but is not a lion. He looks like a lion but is not a one in reality. While Me Jesus Christ I am a true Lion.

A lion is a winner. When he leaves his lair, he works as a winner because he knows that nothing can resist him. He rushes on everything that moves, without fearing anything. He is not afraid of anyone. He is the one who attacks, not the one who defends because all the animals fear him.

As sons and daughters of God, it should have come to your mind that you are also lions like Me. How will the disciple of a Lion not be a lion? But what do I see? Disciples frightened by the pagans. Disciples hiding for fear of what will be said. Do you see the governor's friend living in fear or shyness? On the contrary, he will need everyone to know it in order to take advantage accordingly.

I said, Let the world see your righteous works and glorify My heavenly Father, but I remain unsatisfied. What diploma did Joseph have to save Egypt from seven years of famine? What diploma did David have to kill giant Goliath and deliver Israel from the tyranny of the Philistines? What diploma did Daniel have to be promoted Grand Counsellor of consecutive kings of Babylon, from Nebukadnetsar to Darius the Mede? They had as only diploma My presence. I was present. My presence today is the Holy Spirit who abides in you and with you. See how these heroes were great in their time. My Father was glorified through them. You have in you the greatest diploma of all time: the Holy Spirit. Yes I am with you to triumph. Glorify My Father before the pagans and you will see the glory of God.

I am waiting for Christians to walk with their heads held high, not as if they were hunted by some invisible threat. My disciple must not be ashamed of his faith nor to live by it. It is up to those outside to be afraid because the Holy Spirit convicts them of sin, of justice and of judgment. It's up to the pagans to ask questions, to feel guilty about not knowing Me. The Christian does not have to be afraid like a thief. Be strong and bold! Glorify your Heavenly Father with His Spirit who dwells in you!

Be strong, confident, and bold as lions worthy of the trust of the Lion of the tribe of Judah.

Note: Many face-to-face meetings with the Holy Spirit are expected in the lifetime of a Christian, depending on his level of sanctification. This is the evidence that the Lord Jesus Christ takes very seriously the mission entrusted to the Holy Spirit on earth to Christians. The Christian is therefore invited to maintain his sanctification relentlessly.

Table of contents

9 791094 949115